ghostbread

ghostbread

SONJA LIVINGSTON

The University of Georgia Press *Athens & London*

Paperback edition published in 2010 by
The University of Georgia Press
Athens, Georgia 30602
www.ugapress.org
© 2009 by Sonja Livingston
All rights reserved
Designed by Walton Harris
Set in 10/14 Garamond Premier Pro

Printed digitally in the United States of America

The Library of Congress has cataloged the hardcover
edition of this book as follows:

Livingston, Sonja.
Ghostbread / Sonja Livingston.
ix, 239 p. ; 23 cm. — (Association of Writers and Writing
Programs Award for Creative Nonfiction)
ISBN-13: 978-0-8203-3398-4 (hardcover : alk. paper)
ISBN-10: 0-8203-3398-0 (hardcover : alk. paper)
1. Livingston, Sonja — Childhood and youth. 2. Poor girls —
New York (State) — Biography. I. Title.
HQ777.L58 2009
305.23092 — dc22
[B]   2009009150

Paperback ISBN-13: 978-0-8203-3687-9
          ISBN-10: 0-8203-3687-4

British Library Cataloging-in-Publication Data available

This is a work of literary nonfiction, based on experience and
memory. Only names have been purposefully changed, and then
in deference to those whose lives intersected with my own.

To SONJA MARIE ROSARIO
and all the girls of Rochester, Buffalo,
and places in between

preface

When you pick up a pen, put it to paper, and let yourself go, certain words throw themselves at you, whole paragraphs come to you unbidden, entire passages stake their claim, refuse to be ignored. Even when you don't want them. Especially when you don't want them.

As a girl, I never talked about how I grew up. It was complicated. People might point fingers. My face might turn hot and wet and a hundred shades of red. Mostly, I was certain that I was alone in a way that no one would understand.

But as I sat in my first creative writing class, wadding up paper and waiting for something to come, the stories nudged at me, harder and harder, until finally, they made their way out.

I began to write. Of seven children who followed a mother as she flew around western New York like a misguided bird. How they flew and flew until they were sick from all the flying then landed flat and broken into the muggy slums of Rochester, New York. I wrote of living in apartments and tents and motel rooms. Of places where corn and cabbage grew in great swaths. Of the Iroquois on their reservation outside of Buffalo. About sleeping in shacks and cars and other people's beds, and finally about a tiny dead end street in an overcrowded inner-city neighborhood.

And as I began to share my writing, I learned that I was not so alone. While the specifics of my circumstances were certainly unusual, a child living without basic resources in 1970s America was not as uncommon as I'd once believed.

The western portion of New York State is a coming-together of various influences. The northern tip of Appalachia meets up with the easternmost notch in the Rust Belt. Poverty exists in many forms within a two-hundred-mile radius. It blooms quietly on Indian reservations, in old farm towns, and in cities seething with higher rates of crime and child poverty than New York City. It spreads like a bruise between Buffalo and Rochester, a stain just under the skin.

Writing helped me to talk about the places and people of my childhood and to connect with others, but in sharing, I inevitably encounter someone who does not believe.

"Rochester has no ghetto," they say, or else they cock an eyebrow and say, "Reservations? So near us?"

So we'll get into a car and drive out to a place, only to find that what was once barely standing has finally collapsed. Where for hundreds of years stood a behemoth of a house are now only trees. The old shack that once gave shelter to a brood of children has become vines. The gold-shingled two-story with a gangly lilac out back is just another vacant city lot. And though I can't always recover the specifics (the houses or gardens or trees) of the past, the reality of such existence remains.

It's there. For those who steer their cars off the New York State Thruway and interstates. The broken cities, the sprawling rusted landscapes, the huddled people.

They are all there.

I wrote this book because the pain and power and beauty of childhood inspire me. I wrote it selfishly, to make sense of chaos. I wrote it unselfishly, to bear witness. For houses and gardens and children most of us never see.

acknowledgments

Earlier versions of some material appeared as essays in the *Iowa Review*, *Gulf Coast*, *Puerto del Sol*, and *Mary*.

Many thanks to early readers of my work: Judith Kitchen, Karen DeLaney, Sarah Freligh, Paul Bond, Deb Wolkenberg, Sharon Pierce, and the Hilton HC (Laurie, Bonnie, Donna, Karen R., and Karen K.). I appreciate careful readings by Deanna Ferguson, Allen Galante, Gregory Gerard, Stephen Kuusisto, and Julietta Wolf-Foster. I am grateful to Gail Mott for her thorough reading, and to her and Peter Mott for so much more.

Thanks to my angels from New Orleans, especially Amanda and Joseph Boyden, Dinty W. Moore, Lisa Shillingburg, and Kim Bradley.

Rob McQuilkin, with his sharp eye and quick pen, greatly improved this manuscript and championed it against even greater odds.

Thank you to Kathleen Norris, AWP, and the University of Georgia Press, to family and friends, and most of all, to those represented in these pages.

Much love to Jim.

part one **the get go**

1

I know where I came from.

It must have been April or May of 1967 when he came through town, a vacuum-cleaner salesman with a carload of rubber belts, metal tubing, and suction hoses. Spring in western New York, it was probably a sunless day — he may have been chilled as he grabbed hold of his Kirby upright, walked to the door, and rang the bell.

She was a well-formed redhead with a dry-cleaning job and a house full of children to forget. She must have put hand to hip, flashed falsely shy eyes, and said something about not needing another vacuum.

He had full lips, and used them to throw a smile in her direction. And she, who was partial to full-lipped smiles, let him in.

He rang; she answered. She was hungry; he had a bit of sugar on his finger. He was tired; she provided a pillow for his head. Soft. Sweet. Easy.

Sometimes it's just that simple.

2

I was late. Born in the wrong year, according to my mother. Though scheduled to clear her womb in 1967, I was mule-headed and did not exit my mother's body until late January 1968.

The story was a good one. My mother swore by it. People clucked and laughed when she told it. Growing up, it made my birth seem special. Like I was cracked from another of Adam's ribs or crawled from my mother's womb fully-formed and armored, like some commonplace Athena.

I imagined myself made stronger by all that time inside her. As if twenty-eight extra days and twenty-eight extra nights pressed against the lungs could compensate for the lack of baby pictures, the lack of a proper last name, the lack of a daddy. As if four weeks could ever make such a difference.

We were all late, according to my mother. Except for her first, my brother Will, who was two months early, born backward and twisted. Breach baby. He almost didn't make it, she said. The cord curled round his neck, threatened to pull him back into the womb. Keep him. Will was the only one who'd surprised her — the one whose birth she spoke of with wide eyes and hushed tones. The rest of us were easy — forward-bound, fat-faced, and untangled.

And a month late.

She just carried her babies longer than most, she'd explain if you asked, and if you listened, really listened, you'd understand that it was my mother, not us, who was special — the way her body wouldn't give up its pearls. She'd say it's just a part of who she is, the same way she stopped any watch she wore, all that energy pulsing through her veins. Some things the body just refuses to share.

My mother told the stories of our births over and over, and made them bigger with each telling. We were her handiwork. So she talked about water breaking, the running of fingernails into wood grain, the cutting of umbilical cords. Her tales were rich in gook and detail. Nothing was left out. Except for fathers. They were ghosts that folded themselves into the edges of her tales, vapors that floated in and out of delivery rooms, with us somehow, but never really showing themselves.

3

I had no father, which sounds much more dramatic than it was. If I'd known girls whose daddies held them tight and gazed at them with so much pride it tore at the eyes, I might have thought that all girls should have such a thing. But I never knew such girls. And how can someone miss what she's never had?

No, of this I am sure: a mother was enough.

A mother.

Like mine. One who was smart and pretty and drew horses so well-muscled and real they could gallop off the page. One who came from the state of New Hampshire, where blueberries grew in back of the house her father built and tamaracks stood in lines outside the window. New Hampshire, the granite state, whose bird was the purple finch and flower was the purple lilac and whose motto was live free or die, which is what she'd say if you asked why she made up her own rules about clothes and religion and men.

I'd ask, from time to time, why she didn't do things the way that other mothers did.

"Why don't you have a husband?"

"Why don't you make regular meals?"

"Why don't you teach me to do up my hair?"

In serious moments, I'd ask such questions, and she would listen without showing it, her small hand resting on the spine of a book. I could see by the way she squinted her eyes that she was thinking, so I'd wait until she looked up, eyebrows raised, as though surprised by my presence. As though she'd just remembered me and my questions. She'd look at me hard, and say, "Live free or die — I'm telling you girl, there's no other way to be."

4

My favorite person should have been Carol Johnson. Carol's voice was like gravel, her words came out slow and sifted through the cigarette perpetually pressed between her lips. She was as thick-fingered as any man, but kind. And painfully generous. She had four kids of her own, but managed to treat me like I was special. Carol said beautiful things about my hair and eyes, and when she ran out of things to say, she gave me things. Cupcakes and colored scissors and a glossy black purse with a gold metal snap that she wrapped up for my fifth birthday.

I loved that purse! Its shine and promise. I opened and closed, opened and closed it, delighting in the cushioned clicking of the snap. I clicked it hundreds of times — until I tired of it, or it wore out.

Once the snap lost the hold it had on me, I began to wonder what to fill the purse with. For the first time, I wondered where money came from. I looked into its gaping black mouth and worried over how to feed such a thing. When I asked, my mother laughed.

"Where does money come from?" she cackled. "You be sure and tell me when you find out."

Her laughter did not stop me. I asked my question over and over, until it lost its freshness and earned me only dark stares. I looked into the black interior of the purse and began to see its emptiness as a weight to be carried.

I loved the glossy little accessory, but couldn't enjoy it, and in the end, Carol took the purse back to stop my worrying.

To give and take with such love is rare — so naturally, it was Carol I should have loved most.

Or my mother.

But it was neither. Instead, it was the woman with the owl earrings. A teacher at the day care center who made a seat for me of her lap.

She helped me with my letters and held me for as long as I needed. I'd sit there as often as I could, pushing my head into her chest, looking up at her earrings — silver dangling owls. A few strands of silk-brown hair fell from her ponytail and I'd take them between my fingers while she held me. I'd plop a thumb into my mouth and stare into those earrings. Wise old owls. Silver and jangling. Moving as she laughed.

5

Something big happened.

I found five dollars and discovered what it felt like to swallow the sky. The money was folded on the sidewalk in front of our apartment. I saw its color first, a tight rectangle of green lying flat against the gray walk. It was sitting there like a gift, so I picked it up and handed it over to my mother who thanked me, hugged me, adored me.

"Honestly," she said, "I didn't know how we would eat tonight."

To be taken by the hand to the corner store and allowed to choose a special candy — that's something. To be talked of with gratitude and pleasure, my name coming out of her mouth like a song. To be lifted over the shoulder, made to feel like the sun and the moon — it was almost too much to bear.

But there was a twist. There's always a twist.

Because when things are found, it is also true that they are lost, and the five dollars that made me family hero and benefactress of macaroni and cheese dinner was the very same bill dropped by someone else. So when my mother lifted me up to the counter, I smiled and let my fingers skim the ruffled faces of penny candy, but remembered the Brownie troop that had passed our place just minutes before my find.

I selected my candy reward and thought of the double-file line of brown-uniformed girls, giggling in their cocoa-colored berets, one of them not knowing she'd lost her money, one of them looking, digging perhaps, into her tiny brown pouch the exact moment the atomic fireball settled into my mouth.

6

Finding five dollars wasn't news for long.

Other things happened.

Big things.

Three girls were killed. Right here, in our city. Rochester, New York. They were put into the ground, those girls. Buried under flat stone over at Mount Hope, lying silent beneath the red earth and wild violets of Holy Sepulchre. Something terrible happened to them. Something my mother spoke of with hands over her mouth.

"They were from the city," was all she'd say, "from the city, poor, and Catholic."

Like us.

She never said it, but it was there.

Each had first and last names starting with the same letter. Wanda Walkowicz. Carmen Colon. Michelle Maenza. The man on the news said they were found with half-digested cheeseburgers in their bellies.

Why had those girls let him feed them?

The mystery of their trust plagued me more than the mystery of their deaths. Here's what I decided: I wouldn't eat a thing if he came for me. I knew my letters, could spell out my name, and my mother had told me twice already that my initials were not doubled, so there was that to hold on to. "There's nothing to worry about," my mother said and tried to sound sure of things, but I knew by the way she told us to stay by her side that she was scared too.

One of the girls had lived close to us. Michelle was in the third grade with my brother one day and the next, his classroom had an extra desk.

Lucky for me my initials were mismatched. Good thing my mother mixed things up. And the girls he took were nine or ten, while I was not yet six. Still, he might have run out of double-initialed girls or changed his mind about the age he wanted. I thought of such things, but most of all, I worried about my hunger, that he might sense it in me, that I might forget myself and eat whatever he offered.

So if he came for me, I knew just what to do. I'd decided on the exact cupboard to ball myself into. And if he found me there, I knew how to protect myself. I'd keep my mouth closed, and no matter what — even if he pried it open with big angry hands — I would let nothing pass.

7

Sometimes we'd explore.

My mother and her children walked in a line through the neighborhood, a ragtag group of boys and girls, arranged by descending height. We'd crisscross the streets in the northeast section of the city, resting along the way until we found ourselves on the sloping green hill near the softball field on East Main and Culver. Six kids, grubby-fingered and pushing through the slippery pile of books fished out from the twin Dumpsters that stood like sentries outside the high school. So many gloss-covered books were discarded that they slopped over the tops of the Dumpsters and fell into our hands.

"Who would throw these away?" My mother's eyes grew with the prospect of all those words.

She pushed her red-brown hair into a knot at the back of her neck, sat on the grass, and entered a book so softly that we barely spoke. She only answered after we asked twice if it was okay to chew on purpleheaded clover.

It was warm, with a breeze, and we watched as three Vietnamese men pulled June bugs from the small trees lining the sidewalk. They pulled the bugs from the air, flattened the shells between finger and thumb, then tossed them into the plastic buckets they carried.

"They'll eat those bugs," someone said, and we laughed and chewed the nectar from clover.

We lounged, spread out on the grass until the sun lowered and our skin cooled. Even then, we didn't want to let go of the day and tried lugging armfuls of the books home. In the end, there were not enough hands and arms to carry all those books away. But the want was there.

8

Annmarie VanEpps may as well have been rich.

She had a dollhouse as tall as we were, and though my mother said Annmarie was spoiled, she sometimes let me cross Leighton Avenue to play with the girl and her toys.

My mother was right.

Annmarie was spoiled — but only in the way that poor children can be. She was given things, but they always fell short of what she really wanted. Still, she was the only girl, the youngest, and her mother doted on her in a small and nervous way. Annmarie's mother was tiny. Dark hair curled around a heart-shaped face, and she would have been pretty had she not been so tightly wound, like a hummingbird, moving hard and going nowhere.

In a neighborhood of untucked shirts and mismatched socks, Annmarie and her mother stood out. Her mother wore slacks with creases sharp enough to cut a hand and outfitted her daughter in periwinkle dresses that tied in the back and brought out the blue in Annmarie's eyes.

Annmarie had older brothers, and from them I learned not to play with sticks. One of the VanEpps boys had played with a stick and put a girl's eye out. The girl was left with only one working eye, and after that, whenever any of us picked up a stick and pointed it at a face, my mother would remind us of that poor girl and her nonworking eye. The VanEppses were brought to court by the girl's family, and who knows how that went. It could not have been too damaging, since Annmarie's father had left them years before and other than the oversized dollhouse and a working Lite-Brite, there wasn't much to claim.

9

We had big plans.

We were going camping.

My mother placed an empty cardboard box in the kitchen and once a week deposited some camping essential into it. Toothbrushes and a flashlight one week, pop-up camping cups and a box of matches another. We were planning a big trip. To the Adirondacks, or maybe to New Hampshire, where we'd pick blueberries all day and see what a real mountain looked like. Maybe we'd go back to the house at the foot of Mount Washington. Back to the place my grandfather built, when he was alive and my mother was a girl. Back when the world was as sweet as it ever would be.

10

How to tell it so it's not misunderstood: the hatchet was in her hand and we'd been jumping on beds.

Again.

My mother had told us time and time again not to, but we couldn't resist the cushioned bouncing, the way our hair splashed in the air as we fell. Carol and her kids were visiting and we were bored, so we took to the bed and started bouncing. Then there she was, tight-eyed and in front of us with a hatchet fished out of the camping box.

"In a line," she said, and we made ourselves into a line along the kitchen floor and did what she said because she had a hatchet, and a hardness to her eyes.

"In a line," she said, "jumping."

So we jumped, feeling silly even at our young ages, knowing it was wrong somehow to be forced by hatchet into jumping. But it was no time for joking. My mother's face was red, and though she was looking right at us, she did not seem to see.

She pounded the linoleum with her hatchet, dull side down — jump, jump, jump, she said, and the blade was sharp and her eyes had never been colder and even good old Carol could not calm her and so pretended it was all a joke and told her children to keep jumping in my mother's line.

"Jump, you kids!" my mother said, eyes empty where there was usually blue.

And we jumped. We kept our bodies in flight, feet slapping the floor, faces wet as we sobbed and called out to her to please stop.

Who knows how it ended.

So often, only the beginning of the story remains, like the base of a bridge long gone. We're left with the things we notice as the adrenaline builds — the hairline crack in the floor, the orange and yellow flowered cover on the toaster. So often, the ending does not really matter.

"Jump! Jump! Jump!" she said. And we did.

Until she tired, or our legs gave out, and we fell, ragged, into a pile on the floor.

11

We moved.

Like other people celebrated holidays, we packed our stuff and moved. Leighton Avenue. Bowman Street. East Main Street, upper and lower. All that movement may sound like something, but the places were within blocks of each other and nothing marked the moves as special. In fact, were it not for my mother saying we had a new address, I might not have noticed.

Perhaps they were happy, the moves — our running onto new porches, stretching under sun-filled windows, sitting in front seats of moving vans, fiddling with the loop of keys hanging from the ignition. More likely, though, the moves were nonevents, as moves from one slum apartment to the next tend to be, marked only by a neighbor poking out her head while our olive green sofa was maneuvered through the twists and turns of the entryway, and saying, "Oh, so you all are over here now, hmmm? Well that's all right, it's an okay place, at least you're still close by."

This was the way things were, our moves tiny and circular, until the end of my fifth year, when we packed our belongings and headed out of the neighborhood entirely.

Another move.

But this one was different. We left the small streets that snaked through the northeast quadrant of Rochester. We left Annmarie VanEpps, her bird of a mother, her well-stocked toy box. We left the one-eyed girl, and the empty desk in my brother's classroom. We left the teacher with the owl earrings, Carol and her gift purse, and everything we knew.

This time, we headed west.

West, but it was nothing like a gold rush. Nothing so grand as

California. We didn't even make it out of the state, barely left the county. Still, given our history of movement within the same zip code, the move was big.

The reasons for our leaving were unknown to all but my mother. She just packed up the station wagon and pointed it west. About an hour away. Near Albion, where her cousins had a house and where, it turned out, our camping supplies would come in handy. It was not the Adirondacks, but we pitched a tent in their wide yard and slept beside rows of cow corn. It was not Mount Washington either — no blueberries, no stands of tamarack — but at least there were crickets, and she seemed happy there, my mother, walking up and down the gravel road out front, spending her free time lying on her back, running a flashlight back and forth over the canvas of our green tent.

12

As they often reminded us, the McCullens were not our actual cousins; they were my mother's. But they were relatives nonetheless, and served as hosts for us and our tent until my mother could find a better place.

Aunt Jane was a Jehovah's Witness who had married one McCullen brother, had five girls, then married another and had two more. Polly and Molly were the oldest. Large-bottomed twins with a trail of suds perpetually falling from their ripe hands, the pair was most often found in the kitchen, preparing and eating meals, washing an endless pile of dishes. Linda was heart-faced, golden-haired, and serving time in the local prison for being with a man who'd robbed a store and killed someone in the process. Judith was small and bitter, a prickly weed squatting in the middle of the yard. Tess was a dark and moody tyrant whose magic made even the old barn out back shine with glamour and intrigue. She doled out parts and led us in daily reenactments of *The Wizard of Oz*. Dori was my age and so agreeable she faded from every scene. Tammy, the youngest, was the dark-haired favorite: her pink ruffled bedspread and access to a flush toilet made her a princess, to us.

As a bunch, the McCullens were wildly creative — energy unleashed. Sitting at her electric sewing machine, Aunt Jane would whip off a stream of halter tops to outfit a yard full of sweaty girls. And the stories they told! They laughed and cried as they discussed long dead relatives with children listening from every corner of the room. But the McCullens were also quick to anger, and comfortably aware that their position was much more solid than our own.

Aunt Jane pressured my mother into beating us the time we tried to make cement by peeing in the sand. I felt worse for my mother than for my own behind. She tended to laugh off things like pee-cement, but was in charge of nothing at Aunt Jane's place. I hated my mother's being stuck, the way she finally smacked our bottoms without heart, how even our punishment seemed inadequate compared to the soulful whippings Aunt Jane meted out to her own clan.

13

I wanted Tess to like me.

She was a dark-spirited teenager who talked of kidnappings, the Bermuda Triangle, and the power some people had to bend spoons with their brains. They did this, she said, by thinking hard and wanting it enough.

Tess was the only interesting cousin I had, the sort made more interesting by her rejection of me. Death in general, and ghosts in particular, were big with Tess. She'd burn candles, use the Ouija board, sit Indian-style and call out to John F. Kennedy to "please appear."

"I saw him, I saw him!" she'd cry after looking into the flame of a candle and chanting. And anyone with a voice agreed, though we hadn't caught sight of him, wouldn't even have known what he looked like, would have had an easier time conjuring an Osmond brother than the dead young president. Still, we shot our eyes to the floor and said we saw him too, knowing it was a lie, but saying it because Tess wanted it so badly.

So when she offered to teach me to ride a bike, I had no choice but to agree. In truth, I didn't want to learn, was not as motivated by the prospect of independent travel as some children. More than anything, I did not want to fall.

The bike was bent in places, and finished with the dull paint of houses. Aqua with sea-foam edging. Tess told me to get on and try pedaling.

"I'm afraid," I said.

"Try," was all she said, while crossing her arms over her bony chest.

I wanted to please her, wanted her to like me so much that I'd be given a proper role in the next séance, would be invited as full participant in the next game of Mystery Date. I wanted it, but my legs refused to move. And Tess, who was not given to patience, had used up all the kindness she had access to with her offer to teach me.

So she pushed me.

Hard.

Then screamed for me to pedal, pedal, pedal.

And I did. I rode in a straight line for two full seconds, then banged into the trunk of a thick old maple. The bike's fender was bent even worse than before and I had a fat and bleeding lip, but was proud as I climbed into the station wagon and headed to the Orleans County fair. I replayed the scene from my place on the merry mixers, from the cushioned inside of a bumper car, and from my seat at the very top of the Ferris wheel.

14

The pink took. It was not sweet or giving, as pink should be. The color was fixed to our walls in Albion, the place we moved to after camping out in our cousins' yard. The house my mother found was big and old. White plaster crumbled through the pink walls like whitecaps on a Pepto-Bismol sea. I stared into those breaks night after night. The festering plaster took hold of me; I was a knuckleheaded girl with more time than options, so I stared and stared into those frothy white holes and waited.

Everyone loved Cher. My oldest sister, Lisa, and meanest cousin, Tess, sang her gypsy songs while sashaying under trees. They were girls becoming women, their bodies pained with growth. They had no choice but to dance under dappled leaves, to soak themselves in the black-magic salve of Cher. And though my own body was far from womanhood, I needed her too, that buck-skinned woman looking out to me from the top of a lopsided pile of my mother's music. Cher was radiant astride her palomino and cool even in the desert heat. At night, she'd leap from her album cover and come for me on that very same horse, entering my room through an opening in the crumbling walls.

First came the gallop, hooves sounding with heartbeat swish and rhythm. Then her. Glowing, shining, a sword of light, a stream of hair following crescent moon eyes as she scooped me up from the bed I shared with two or three sisters and my mother. She'd shake me gently, call me "little bird." And off we'd fly. To the dusty mountain pass of her album cover, to the blinding glitter of Hollywood, or to anyplace else that ginger-soft horse would take us.

15

On warm nights, the family spread throughout the house like lounging cats. But when it was cold, we slept in the same room, the pink room being the only one with heat. My mother and her six children gathered hungrily around the large furnace that squatted in the center of the room. Some shared a big bed, others slept on the floor; it was like camping out in our cousins' yard, only warmer.

There was no working bathroom in the house. We had a small room complete with tub and toilet, but no pipes were attached to either. It was simply a room to wander into and wonder over. But for bathroom services, we used the outhouse behind the house. Sometimes we'd drag the old claw-foot tub, like a porcelain bear, into the living room, where we'd plug the drain and fill it with water heated on the kitchen stove, then hop into it in twos and threes.

I got a twin bed once, for some occasion or because my mother found one at a good price. I had it for about two days, but lost it when I peed on purpose. I was afraid to go to the outhouse alone, so I peed right on the bed, right through the Raggedy Ann and Andy sheet set. The mattress had a plastic sheath whose protective powers intrigued me and which I convinced myself I was testing, but mainly, I was afraid of the spiders that spun on silver strands along the outhouse path. Someone saw the wet sheets, and I was found out. And so, as punishment for my freestyle peeing, the secondhand bed and its new mattresses — even the pee-stained sheets — were taken from me and given to my sister Stephanie, while I got Steph's old sleeping bag. I cried hard about losing my bed, but in the end, I didn't miss it, and was somehow comforted by my return to the floor.

The house had once been a stop for stagecoaches, but by the time we arrived, it was divided into two large apartments. People moved in and out of the other apartment all the time, as though stagecoaches still pulled through — made stops, loaded up, then pulled off again. Brothers, sisters, cousins, and friends stepped down from unseen coaches, stayed awhile, then packed up again, left. People were here and not here, in a ghostly procession of comings and goings. Except men. There were no fathers or boyfriends in either apartment.

A young woman lived upstairs. If she had a husband, he had wronged her, or died. The scent of male tragedy clung to her. She painted her toenails red, wore ankle bracelets, and drove without shoes. My mother, who painted no part of her body, pointed out that barefoot driving was illegal.

The woman had several cats and gave me one of the tiniest, a kitten so soft and white I named her Fluff. She was warm, I was cold: that was the basis of our love. My mother warned me about holding the cat, said she'd die if I didn't let her be, that I'd make her sick by carrying her around so much. But I couldn't stop. I was crazy with desire for Fluff, and nuzzled my face into her fur every chance I got.

16

Albion is in Orleans County, one of the poorest counties in New York State. And in the poorest of counties, the poorest of people came from West Virginia, though the reason for their northern migration was unclear. Perhaps they'd simply followed the eastern tip of Lake Erie up through Pennsylvania till it washed them to the southern shore of Lake Ontario where they could go no further. Or else they came to pull fruit from freckled branches, to cut the blue-green balls of cabbage that grew in lines close to the earth. Or maybe they knew something special about the place, some secret or well-disguised potential.

Mrs. Drake was a West Virginian, and moved into the upstairs apartment after it was vacated by the woman who'd worn her sadness like a perfume. Mrs. Drake was old. A clutch of nappy gray hairs sprang from her head so that she looked like a dandelion gone to seed. Small as a girl, Mrs. Drake had a voice that sounded like the yellow paper I helped scrape from her worn kitchen walls. She repapered the small room with my mother's collection of newspapers from the day JFK had been killed. My mother, shocked at seeing the headlines she'd been saving glued to walls, couldn't make sense of Mrs. Drake's crazy ways. She saw her as a bug of a woman. But I was mystified. Nothing was off limits to Mrs. Drake, not someone else's belongings, not the eating of weeds, not indelicate bits of personal advice. That was her main appeal.

"Listen up, baby — you ever getcha an ear infection, jes' get yourself some sheep's urine, soak it up with cotton balls, an' stuff the whole mess up inta your ear — it'll clear things out in no time."

Mrs. Drake picked wildflowers from the field out back and boiled them into remedies. For Christmas, she gave each of us four girls a smooth-handled wooden mirror. She served hot tea and told stories while teaching me to braid a long line of yarn with a stubby crochet hook.

17

The backyard was the flattened acres of abandoned farms with a few clumps of trees left here and there. We built a fort in one of those tree stands, an oasis amid tall grasses and weeds. Whole days unwound there. We hung from homemade swings, chewed on monkey vines, told big stories about the land, saying that some child had died in the bottomless pond out back. We imagined quicksand in those places where no one but our bravest brother, Anthony, ever ventured.

Anthony stole rides on Mr. Stragg's horses. Mr. Stragg owned the house and the land. He lived in a small ranch-style house built to the side of the clapboard giant in which we lived. His face was waxed and red — a glistening turnip — and when they came, his words were mangled and choked, as though sifted through a wad of burlap in his throat. A farmer paid by the government not to farm, Mr. Stragg was quietly kind, my mother told me years later, and left groceries on our steps when he knew we had nothing. But in Albion, all I knew was that Mr. Stragg was crotchety and preoccupied and not to be pestered.

His wife was sick, her body curled into a wiry gray ball. When things got quiet, she'd surprise everyone. She'd have a fit, unwind herself, claw the clothing from her body, then run wild and naked from her bed. She required constant care. To add to Mr. Stragg's troubles, Anthony would not stay off the horses kept out back, horses that Mr. Stragg had clearly stated were not for riding.

Our mother begged Tony not to and punished him when he did, but the temptation to feel acres pounding underfoot, the soft power of the horse in his hands, the tall grass at his heels, the wind at his back — these things proved too much for Anthony, who hopped onto those horses' backs whenever someone wasn't looking.

18

The fields out back were loaded with strawberries, which we picked and ate in bowls with milk. My mother also boiled them into jams and jellies. We grew vegetables in a muck garden near the house. Carrots, lettuce, and tomatoes mainly. We ate homegrown vegetables and fruits in season, and otherwise survived on the foods my mother canned. Homemade pickles, peaches poured into cobblers, strawberry preserves scooped onto warm biscuits.

My mother stored her peaches and beans in mason jars high up in a pantry that was too large to fill. The pantry a room of its own practically, with scalable shelves layered in thick enamel. The shelves were soft from a century of springtime paintings, the surface so giving my fingernails left half-moon imprints on its skin as I climbed.

19

In September, a school bus stopped in front of the house and took us to Albion Primary and Secondary schools. The driver was thick-featured and rarely moved from his cushioned perch, except on holidays, when he handed out treats from a plain brown bag — candy canes at Christmas, red wax lips on Halloween.

One day after leaving the bus, my oldest sister cried. While the rest of us bawled as needed, Lisa was more stone than girl, her face never crumpling to tears. I kept my eyes on her, and followed close. As we watched for cars and crossed the road to the house, I asked why. She walked away. Fast. Her face was hard and wet.

"Why are you crying?"

"The kids were picking on us," she said, and pushed away. Lisa was mean, but my curiosity about what had broken her was bigger than my fear, so I followed.

"Why would they pick on us?" I asked. Why? Why? Why?

"Why do you think?" She lashed out like a whip of salted ocean spit. "Our house is ugly, our clothes are shit — they hate us because we're poor!" She let it all out in one angry sob, then ran into the house.

Before that day, I'd been sent home with boxes of donated clothes from a teacher in the primary school a few times. I had always felt happy with my oversized loads, feeling proud to have been trusted with a special cargo. But after Lisa's crying, I refused the boxes; I lied, made excuses.

I once opened one of those boxes. Back before my sister cried. Back when I still took them. During a slow ride on the school bus, I broke through a wide strip of tape and pushed my fingers into a small pot of solid perfume. I oiled my finger, rubbed the scent of jasmine blossoms onto my wrist and felt pretty.

20

At school, I learned to read and write and use spit in creative ways. I had a crush on a sweet-faced boy who looked like Randy from the Jackson Five. "Rhinestone Cowboy" was the big song. At school, I shined. Other than having the silver dollar that had been left by the tooth fairy stolen from the coat closet during recess, I loved school; it was big and bright, a gem in my pocket. Everything was just right. Until Zaida.

Zaida was the only girl poorer than me, and in an effort to be more like them and less like her, I agreed to help the other girls put a tack on her seat, pretend-laughing as she lowered her bony behind onto it.

Days later, my mother steered the car out to Zaida's house. Sober rows of zucchini and eggplant lined both sides of the shack whose paint had faded and run gray. My mother shocked me by not only knowing Zaida's family, but by stopping to drop off something for them.

The skinny girl with the apron dress and crane legs stood still as a giant bird in her dusty yard and did not look my way when my mother mentioned our being in the same grade. The air between us pulsed, though no one else seemed to notice. She flickered a bit, then faded; looking as tired as the dirt at her feet.

As we pulled away, I felt some of Zaida's grit. Inside me. Grit and shame and dust. It got inside, and stayed.

21

We'd return to the city on some holidays, but usually stayed in the big old house in Albion where we'd gather around the heat and make the most of whatever day was to be celebrated.

We didn't trick-or-treat on Halloween because the houses were so far from each other. Instead, our mother asked questions about past presidents or spun the globe and had us locate Istanbul or Uruguay. In exchange, we'd receive thick candy bars, with the game rigged to make sure everyone received equal doses of chocolate.

For Christmas, Steph and I received twin dolls. The closest in age, we always got different versions of the same thing. Same winter coat, different color. Same dress, different pattern. She got the George doll, I got Georgina. Both of them were three feet tall with pink grins plastered on their faces. Their milk-white skin was sprayed with freckles and crowned with red hair. But no matter how charming their scrubbed Gaelic features may have been to some, their green-eyed, button-nosed look was the one that none of us had. As a result, and in a sole attempt at unity, we were repelled by the sweet-faced pair. Still, I didn't hate Georgina the way that Steph hated George. The fact was, she despised dolls altogether, and was endlessly irritated by my mother's sloppy inattention to this detail.

"Oh Steph," my mother said, puffing out disclaimers like other mothers blew out silky loops of smoke — "I forgot about you and dolls."

Another Christmas and she'd meet Steph halfway, get her a GI Joe. But there was no compromise in Albion, when Steph still hoped that every unwrapped gift would be the Erector set she'd never get. Unable to shake the disappointment of getting a doll, Steph refused to touch George at all until that spring when she beheaded him and hung his ugly red head from the treehouse perch. I cried, though in truth, I wasn't so much mourning the doll as grieving the loss of the pair. Georgina was nothing without George.

22

One frozen blue evening, we took rides on a horse-drawn sleigh. A man came to the house and gathered us by the load, our laughter the only sound for miles. Looking up through the warmth of a scarf that covered everything but my eyes, I saw a sky that bloomed velvet flowers. Back and forth, the man took us along Route 31A, while those not in the sleigh clamored by the open door, our hot breath gunning fog as we begged for another run.

The sleigh was decked in bells with holly boughs tied to its side. Or perhaps the driver just seemed festive. He liked my mother. Or owed her something. It all ended, however, when his horses and sleigh ran off the road into an icy ditch. My mother was harsh to him then. She shut us up inside, left him out in the cold.

"He's drunk," she said, an unusual air of judgment darkening her voice.

"Therese — Therese, Therese," the sleigh driver called, "I can get her up and running again — I can, I can."

Pound. Pound. Pounding on the door.

"Therese, Therese. . . ." he called after her from the frozen side of the door, joined with us at not wanting the fun to end. But she just stood there, silent. She would not look at us. She would not be swayed.

23

My mother worked in a gypsum factory just outside Batavia. The world passed from night to day and back again as she laced electrical wires through drywall boards. The only woman to work in the prefab metal building, she learned to drink coffee in hollow rooms with sawdust-laden floors. Every now and then, she had a day off, and I'd manage to fake sick to gain trips to Carrol's for burgers, to the downtown diner for grilled cheese, to Ames for stiffly coordinated outfits stuck to plastic hangers. Those rare stolen days were such a treat that I had to remind myself to appear sick. Filling up on green glass bottles of ginger ale, I let the bubbles tickle my throat on the way down to a stomach already very much at peace.

24

We were Catholic, but only in Rochester. I was never sure if it was due to fewer churches to choose from in Albion, or simply the more relaxed attitude toward religion that wide-open fields encouraged, but we only attended church on return trips to the city.

Once, at Sunday school, while coloring in Adam, Eve, and the Snake on black-outlined sheets, someone asked about how the original pair, living outdoors, went to the bathroom. I knew how, so I raised my hand and told the nuns about our outhouse. They didn't believe. I insisted, told them about the black-eyed Susans and buttercups that grew on the path leading up to it. I left out the spiders, tried to make it sound pretty. Like Eden. The other kids laughed, and the nuns bristled. When my mother arrived, they spoke to her in hushes until she became red in the face. She'd never been so ashamed, she whispered not quite to me, on the drive home.

My grandmother visited in Albion, one of only two visits with her I'd ever had. A stranger to me, she won my affection by giving me a bracelet strung with bits of shell and glass. I had never owned anything so lovely. It was from somewhere warm, which I kept saying was Hawaii, though my mother corrected me that this was not the case. Probably it came from Florida. Or Vegas.

My grandmother was not like other grandmothers. She moved from place to place and drank whiskey like water. Besides the fact that my usually laughing mother became silent in her presence, I knew only five things about my grandmother: (1) her name was Anna Mae — first Jackman, then Baker, finally DeFrank; (2) she sewed my sister Lisa's lace communion dress and matching veil by hand; (3) once, when we were still in the city, she'd left eight wrapped gifts for our eight Michigan cousins without any for us, and as soon as she pulled away, my mother simply tore away the eight Michigan names and gave the gifts to us; (4) she sprinkled salt on her apples and taught me to do the same, which tasted bitter, but I pretended was the best thing ever, if only to earn her admiration; (5) she was a hard woman, not given to admiration.

25

Will was the oldest in the family, the quiet one who, because of his age, his silence, and the fact that he'd spent the past year living with his father in Albany, was basically a stranger. In fact, by the time things went bad between he and his father, and he arrived in Albion, I had nearly forgotten about him. Thin and quiet, Will kept to himself, was shy with even my mother. He had been just a name while he was gone, a ghost really, and he remained one once he returned home — wandering from room to room without a word. Only a creak in the floorboard or a muffled sneeze would remind us he was there.

Will was in high school and worked at the Swan Library, a job that I had no ability to hold but was jealous of just the same. All those books. When I was fortunate enough to get inside, I'd look through the shelves in the big old building, thinking how unfair it was that Will not only got to be around them so often, but was actually paid for it.

A monk from the library brought Will to his house and stuffed him with sweets. Intrigued by the old man and his fancy home, we begged to go inside for visits when it was time to pick Will up. Sometimes my mother said yes and ran errands while we combed the red velvet cushions of his antique chairs with our fingers.

White as the sugar waffles he always served, the monk told horrible stories while we gathered at his feet, eating caramels by the bagful and dipping our fingers into the powdered remains of those delicate waffles. He'd lean into us and screw up his face, telling us about three sisters who'd stayed out late at a party one night. He'd take his time with his stories, noting how the youngest had hair so blonde it shone in the sunlight and how each of the girls had dressed for bed in gowns of pink and gold and kissed each other goodnight.

"The only problem," he said in a quiet voice, bringing his white lips close to our foreheads as he spoke, "was that they forgot to lock their doors that night."

The girls in his stories were always stalked and attacked, their heads cut from the neck. The losing of heads should have ended things, of course, but the monk never stopped there. Heads could be reattached with a well-placed scarf or a pearl choker necklace, he told us, so that his story became one of girls trying to protect the remaining sanctity of their necks. For they truly only lost their heads when they allowed someone too close.

This is what I learned from the monk, as I munched on sweets and swallowed his tales: No matter how smart or how pretty, girls were always conquered in the end. They'd forget their caution, allow some well-intentioned man to unclasp a cameo choker or blue silk scarf, and heads would tumble.

Despite the monk (or because of him) I learned to like scary stories. In fact, my mother came to count on me as her companion for the creepy television shows that only she and I liked. Mainly they were detective shows like *The Night Stalker* or low-budget horror films involving some form of vegetation gone mad with desire for human blood.

At times she drew an arbitrary line and said I was too young to see a particular show. She did this when *Rosemary's Baby* came on TV. No matter how I begged, my mother insisted on watching Rosemary and her devil-baby alone. Certain that I had been wronged, I could not let go and stayed up soaking in whatever blurred sounds of poison-malted shakes and satanic chanting I could manage to catch from the other room. I fell asleep that night, triumphant, listening to Rosemary's screams.

26

Green shoots poked through the melting earth.

Snowdrops, my mother said. She knew about flowers and liked to tell us about them. Sometimes she'd talk about other things. On a sunny day in spring, she shared a secret.

"I'm pregnant," she said, while lying on her side in tight blue jeans, all curves as she informed her children that another was on the way.

A baby! I heard the words and curled into her side. I touched my mother's denim-clad leg, wrapped both arms around the fullness of her upper thigh.

"A baby," I said.

"Yes," came her voice, "but not for a while, though."

I closed my eyes and began to imagine the soft skin, the sweet-smelling hair. I had baby dolls, of course, and a younger sister already, but at five, Mallory was too big to wrap into a blanket and carry around. A baby, I thought again, imagining the ruffled clothes and bottles of white talcum. A real baby, I thought, and began to feel as though I might rise up off the mattress and float. In fact, I may have risen to the ceiling with happiness, but I checked myself — I had learned the foolishness of letting go before cutting my first tooth. My mother had always swelled with promise, talked of milk and honey, but was as hard to hold on to as the wind. Remembering this, I pulled myself back to the reality of the overcrowded mattress.

Pulling away a thick wave of cinnamon hair as she spoke, she looked into our faces to make sure we heard.

"We'll have to give the baby away," she said.

27

I hated Peg and Leroy.

They were strangers pretending to be friends because my mother was giving them the baby. Our baby, who was going to be half-Indian, my mother had told us, like Cher.

Stringy clumps of hair the color of strained carrots twined round Peg's thin neck. The chalky line of her lips receded into a small chapped face. Eager to show that they liked kids, they chose me to spend the day at their house, a house that smelled of Pine-Sol and too much scrubbing. Lacy afghans of brown and orange draped the backs of plaid couches. The place was quiet, with no books or toys. I fell into a chair and waited for time to pass.

I left the chair only to accompany them to the grocery store, where Peg bought me a pack of barrettes — a plastic-wrapped row of twelve hair clips, the kind clipped to the shiny heads of pretty girls at school.

Wow, I thought, maybe Peg is not so bad after all.

I pushed a banana-yellow barrette into my hair and took a nap near an open window, clutching the prize of the others. When I woke, the barrettes were gone. I ran downstairs. My fingers raced back and forth under a hedge of prickly shrubs. Back and forth. Back and forth. Until my hands were rubbed raw by privet and holly.

The barrettes were not to be found. Peg, of course, thought I'd thrown them away, became enraged when I told her I couldn't find them; her face snapped shut. Leroy, who was little more than the red beard that masked his face, comforted her with a steady hand to the shoulder. They drove me home in silence, and as soon as my mother opened the door, Peg told her about the barrettes. She heated up as she spoke, said how ungrateful I was. I ran to my mother, turned to Peg, and screamed that I hated her. When the redheaded woman did not flinch, I went further.

"And you're never gonna get our baby!"

My mother dug into my skin with her hands, told me to shut up, while Peg hissed, then buried her head into Leroy's flannelled chest and cried.

28

We kept her.

My mother decided that Lynne would be her middle name, and allowed us to vote on the first. Rachel or Amy.

"Rachel means little lamb," my mother said.

I sensed her nudging us toward the name, but I chose Rachel primarily on account of a girl named Amy in my class with a tiny row of rotted teeth.

As the weeks went by, my mother's stomach pushed the limits of her clothing. Her auburn hair grew thick and curled around her face like a wild crown.

We watched, intent on the mystery of another of us growing inside her body. We watched, and life continued around us.

29

My cousin Judith cut my hair off one day while my mother was at work.

"I wanted practice cutting, and the shag is in style," she said when my mother walked through the door and stood staring at the strands of hair drying on the floor.

Judith was unapologetic as she twisted her body into my mother's and explained the haircut. Underweight and eyes bulging, Judith looked like a stray cat, but instead of telling her to scat, my mother said nothing. She simply took us home and did not speak for hours. The razor cut was so short it stood up on top. My mother could not look at it. Could not look at me. I must have looked as ragged as we were.

Hating to see my mother broken, I blamed myself for having trusted Judith's touch. She had always been cold, the words that came out of her mouth clanged like metal on glass. I had never really liked her, and so, when she agreed in advance to baby-sit while my mother went to the hospital to have the baby, I cried.

One day, my mother tripped on a toy, and her water broke. The next day Judith was walking around the house, barking orders, and reclining on my mother's big bed in the cool-weather bedroom.

Judith sat under the white chenille bedspread, the TV set planted squarely before her. When she noticed me watching, she said it was late and told me to get to bed. I said that my mother always let me watch *The Sonny & Cher Show*. She said no. When I did not budge, Judith reminded me that my mother was not there. Still, I remained by the side of the bed.

Judith was tired and mean, but I was pigheaded and right.

"I am allowed to watch Sonny and Cher, I am!" I chanted, as if it were a prayer, until Judith could stand it no longer and dialed my mother at the hospital.

A minute into the call, Judith's hand loosened on the receiver, her eyes flipped to the ceiling, and I knew that my mother had backed me up.

Judith did not let go of power easily, though. Hanging up the phone, she swore under her breath and said that I was spoiled. She was wrong, of course; my mother spoiled no one. Still, she had given me victory over Judith, and though I didn't want to be near my bitter second cousin as she sprawled her scrawny body under my mother's covers, I sat on the edge of the bed and made myself watch the entire show. I was tired, but sat there straight-backed till Sonny and Cher sang "I Got You Babe," their closing song.

The pair exchanged wet glances with each other and then with the viewing audience. That night, Chastity joined her parents on stage. Cher was jubilant at the arrival of her daughter, and beamed as though the sun had been harnessed and brought before her. She sparkled and glowed and squeezed her daughter's hand. Finally, Cher broke into a wide smile and blew all of America a kiss goodnight. Then she took her baby into her arms and turned to leave — the beads of her glassy gown swirling about her feet as they walked off stage.

When all signs of Cher had vanished, after she'd returned to the shimmer of her Hollywood life, I walked back to the big room and laid myself down. It was dark, but the walls were stubborn, and I could still make out the pink. The pink I spent too much time looking into. The hard broken pink. I stared into the broken plaster holes and waited.

30

The thing was, it had a dent in it. A scar ran across the face of the metal box. It was chipped and rusted in spots, pushed inward, and pressed together whatever unfortunate food item was placed inside.

There was nothing pretty about my lunchbox, nothing to see but the huge old head of Kwai Chang Caine, the crime-fighting monk from TV. And if you looked at it, that's all you'd see — Caine's bald head, cracked by the dent, looking like the shell of an overcooked egg.

The dent was there long before I ever got hold of it. It was a hand-me-down from my oldest brother, Will, who was as strange as the box.

And don't think I didn't try covering Kung Fu's rocky head with a carefully placed hand or two. I tried. And tried. But his head ballooned and was way too wide for covering. I was convinced that the head was the first thing people noticed about me on the bus to Albion Primary School or at the Brownies. Having the head of Muhammad Ali or Evel Knievel — even the entire Walton family, including John-Boy and his squishy red mole — would have been far less painful.

I never told my mother how much I hated it, not wanting to seem weak. I preferred to be seen as greedy and begged regularly for a Josie and the Pussycats box. And when begging didn't work, I banged my own head against Kung Fu's on the school bus, the first time by accident, but after that, for the easy laughs it garnered, and the chance of damaging it beyond repair. And when knocking heads with Kwai Chang Caine failed to ruin the box, I simply left it at home and waited to eat my lunch till after school.

On those autumn nights when flocks of Brownies gathered in fidgety groups in the school gymnasium and opened their sewing boxes in search of thread and needle to fashion dolls from empty Palmolive bottles, I'd look shocked that my own box had gone missing and ask my cousin Dori for a needle and some thread.

"Where's your sewing kit?" my mother asked when the troop leader reported that I'd forgotten it yet again and had to borrow from Dori, whose box was everything a sewing kit should have been — clear plastic with powder-yellow handles, stuffed to capacity with yarn and thread and a rainbow of fabric scraps.

I shrugged and kept to myself the fact that mine was not even a real sewing kit, that I would have preferred to pull needle and thread from a brown paper bag than carry around sewing supplies in Kung Fu's big buttery head. I said nothing, and kept as a secondary source of shame the fact that I cared about such things.

I decided to be rid of it once and for all by convincing my mother that I hated Brownies. And either she was sick of coming up with money for dues or I was an excellent liar, because my mother somehow believed that I no longer wanted to sing and sew and dip peeled apples into brown sugar and cinnamon, push them onto the ends of broken branches, then turn them over an open fire.

I hated the songs and the parades, I said, and prayed she wouldn't look into my eyes.

"Let me quit," I pleaded.

And just like that, she did.

My mother had other things on her mind. A new baby to feed, a sitter to pay, a job to hold on to. And boxes to pack. We'd lived in Albion for three years — a tiny eternity given our record — but we were heading out again.

Our stay in the crumbling old house was over. Time at play in the strawberry patches out back, hours hiding in tall grass and cow corn, late-night walks along the outhouse path with my bravest sister in hand — all of this was coming to an end.

31

With little explanation and no preparation, most of us moved onto the Tonawanda Indian Reservation. The reservation was south of Albion, closer to Buffalo. The three oldest kids (Will, Anthony, and Lisa) were either sent back to Rochester to stay with friends, or took a train to stay with their father in Albany. In truth, I hardly noticed. So many people crowded around the edges of our murky family, it was hard to keep track of who was there or not.

As we drove onto reservation land, we looked for teepees and tomahawks, but were greeted only by long stretches of trees and, between them, small houses that leaned softly into the earth.

"There are no teepees," my mother said as she steered the car down the winding roads into the heart of the reservation where faces browner than those of the Indians on TV peeked out from passing yards. "The Iroquois built long houses, not teepees."

My newest sister was half-Indian. Rachel's father was a Seneca and from the reservation. Billie was his sister and friendly with my mother, so we'd be staying at her place.

Billie's hair hung long and black and flapped against her large behind as she walked through the one-bedroom home that on any given night held ten to fifteen people. Jolie, Lana, and Soupy were Billie's children and thus the rightful inhabitants of the tiny house. Soupy was the youngest, a fat-faced boy of four whose real name had been discarded the day he was said to have fallen into a huge pot of soup — emerging from the pot baptized in venison broth, and with a new name.

Lana lied. I learned this within hours. She told everyone I'd wet the bed that very first night. Shy because my mother wasn't around, I didn't call Lana a liar, and just shook my head back and forth, staring at the dark spot on the thinly-sheeted sagging mattress that had held both our bellies the night before. I couldn't believe how she lied. I wanted to cry, but didn't let myself. Lana's eyes were hot and mean; she used them like pokers.

"Forget Lana," Jolie said, "that's just how she is."

Jolie was the oldest. At nine, she was one year older than me and so pretty it hurt. Grown-ups evaluated children's beauty as though they weren't in the room and Jolie, they said, was just gorgeous. Her hair had a bit of curl, a beauty mark hovered over her top lip, and her skin was the color of cream because her father was Italian. Italian, and in prison. Lana and Soupy's skin, on the other hand, was as chocolate as Billie's. Their father was not Italian but was in Attica just the same.

Jolie embraced me, was as friendly as Lana was mean. Right after Lana's accusation, she took me to the reservation candy store — a locked shack in the woods near the home of the old man who owned it. I followed Jolie up his porch steps.

"He's a chief," she whispered as she set her hand to the door.

He answered her knocking with a clouded stare. Blue at the edges, his black eyes pushed past me. He asked Jolie where she got the paleface. Jolie shrugged. I whipped round to see what type of thing a paleface was, and when I saw nothing, slowly understood that the old man with ponytailed white hair must mean me.

I was the paleface.

"We came for candy," Jolie said.

He waited a minute, so that we were not sure if he'd even heard, then disappeared into the house. Except for the sound of cushioned feet on the floor, it was utterly quiet; I imagined moccasins touching down on moss-green carpet. He returned with a loop of keys, and I noticed that his lined face was the same maple syrup color as Jolie's. I shifted my weight and stared at the sandals strapped to my feet.

"Not her," he said, pointing to be sure we both understood. Still, I followed them over to the shack just beyond his house, pretended the words had somehow been a mistake, and pretended the old man's voice had not sounded like an axe chopping wood. When we reached the door, I turned away and handed Jolie my quarter, sneaking peeks through the torn mesh of the screen as I waited. Rows and rows of Sweetarts and candy cigarettes and plastic fruit filled with flavored sugar lined the shelves. Jolie pointed at each candy option and looked out the door to see if that's the kind I wanted, eventually emerging with hands full.

The walk back to Billie's was quieter. Before, our words had tumbled into each other as we talked of strawberry lip gloss and KC and the Sunshine Band. On the way home, I noticed that crickets had begun to sound. I tried counting tiger lilies but couldn't stand to look into their spotted interiors. The velvet insides, I couldn't help thinking, robbed the trumpeted weeds of their beauty; their spots reminded me of snakes.

32

When you eat soup every night, thoughts of bread get you through.

Bowl after worn plastic bowl of unfocused ingredients floated before me in a strained broth. Corn, carrots, cabbage, and whatever else could be found were softened in water and flavored with animal fat. We had soup on the reservation every day, sometimes twice. The overworked broth was even further weakened by the knowledge that my mother worked in a factory and had money for Beefaroni. She said that eating Beefaroni would be rude, with Billie and her kids eating soup. I thought about sleeping on the floor while Billie's family slept on beds and couldn't understand.

My bread craving grew.

Cold mornings, I spooned cornmeal mush into my mouth, thankful for at least something warm that was not soup. Warm and solid, the mush was sweetened with a trace of syrup. Still, mush was mush, and nowhere near as solid as bread. Bread was what I wanted.

33

In September, we were bussed a few towns away for school. Brown eyes settled upon us as we climbed aboard. My sisters and I were the only whites on the bus, and in the days to come, I would fight almost daily with a dark girl who insisted on making fun of my whiteness. Neither of us wanted to fight, but she had to say things, and I had to defend myself. I was only eight years old, but I knew this. I learned to say just enough to avoid a fight without seeming weak. She did the same. Leaning into me, she said she couldn't wait for the day to kick my white ass. I made my face stiff and talked about how good it would be to kick her Indian ass once and for all while praying it would never come to that. Despite our talk, however, we always sat near the other, sometimes even slipping into the same wide seat.

Winding its way through broken roads, beyond Indian land, the bus headed west, to the town of Akron. Except for our busload of Senecas, the school was filled with whites, and a place I hoped to escape notice. And for a few minutes anyway, it appeared I would. Until the teacher called my name on the first day of school.

"Please stand when your name is called," came the voice from the front of the room, and I obeyed, not noticing until I had stood that every other child standing was brown. The teacher walked to her desk and returned with a pile of school supplies, which were passed into open hands. Free supplies, I thought, this can't be so bad. The colored pencils, in particular, caught my eye. But when the teacher came to me, she squinted. She looked into my blue eyes, scanned my light brown hair, rechecked the names on her list, looked back into my face, then returned to her list. In the end, she decided against my eligibility, asked me to sit back down, while the colored pencils I'd come to think of as my own remained on the corner of her desk.

By Christmas, Billie's house had become home. Snow grew deep, water became ice. Deer carcasses had long since disappeared from trees. And though my mother warned against wanting too much, I wanted ice skates for Christmas. I wanted them like I wanted bread. Only I got the skates. I opened the gift and it was like magic. Had I hovered above and watched as the red foil paper was torn from the box, I would have been startled by the look of joy on my own face. Like my teacher, I would have blinked, scanned my face, and had to look again. I would have thought I was seeing a hot cocoa commercial or an after-school special about poor kids and Christmas miracles as this joyful imposter of myself removed the lid of the box and lifted out a brand-new pair of skates. Years later I discovered that my brother's saxophone had been sold to buy presents that year, but at the time I was ignorant of such things, and pushed my feet into the skates without guilt.

After the gifts were opened, all the kids grabbed their skates and headed out to the ice, except for my sisters, who had neither asked for nor received skates. Steph followed the crowd to the frozen pond where I skated in circles, my scarf flapping in the wind as I laughed. It was the best day ever. Cold snapped my face red and, as I began to glide, I still felt something of the hot cocoa commercial. Steph sat at the edge on a pile of snow. Watching. She was my best sister, but I barely even heard as she asked to try out the skates.

"Wait — just another couple minutes, okay?" I said again and again as I whipped round and round the frozen pond.

I couldn't stop. In plain sight of the dark-haired girl who always finished the soup I couldn't eat and killed bugs for me and lent her mittens when mine had holes or were lost, I couldn't stop. Those skates carried me across the pond like the wind pushing a leaf along the road.

My cheeks must have been red circles and there was the scent of hot cocoa and it was magnificent, so I managed not to see her.

"Can I try now?"

Day became night, and just before the call for home, as everyone else was getting back into boots, I remembered my frozen sister, removed a skate, and gave it to her. I loved my sister better than anyone, but need must be bigger than love, because even then, I couldn't bear to give up both skates. Steph quietly settled for one, and the two of us flopped on the ice for a few cold minutes before heading home.

34

Mallory was younger than me, but not the youngest. Rachel was the baby, the dark-haired reason for our move to the reservation. Mallory was blonde with ringlets and dimples. The truth was I'd never quite forgiven her for being born, but due to limited options I'd sometimes play with her.

Everyone loved Mal. They couldn't get over how adorable she was. "Ooh, look at her — she's an angel, just like a little Shirley Temple."

Everyone said it. Even those who didn't like whites thought she was a doll. Perhaps she was so pale that she seemed less pale, her golden curls and pink cheeks putting her in a fairytale category.

People played Shirley Temple songs and Mallory danced to them. They laughed and clapped. They thought this was cute. I thought it was stupid, though I found myself wanting to be asked to dance and sing, too. On New Year's Eve, the adults dropped off one at a time, either leaving or passing out. Mal and I were in the kitchen, standing on chairs. The record player was perched high up on a shelf, and we took turns dragging the needle back to the same song. Over and over. We listened to "The Good Ship Lollipop." With the adults asleep and Mallory still in first grade, I made the rules, and the first thing I decided was that yellow ringlets hardly mattered. Girls with flat brown hair could sing golden songs, too. There were bottles of vodka and schnapps on the table. I danced and twirled in the tiny kitchen. I sang Shirley Temple songs at the top of my lungs. I let peppermint schnapps trickle down the back of my throat and felt fire come up from my belly.

35

Billie's house was as small as a shack to begin with, but as the wind whipped east from Lake Erie and south from Ontario, we crouched in its hold so that, by late February, we began to feel cramped. Even as we gathered around the wood-burning stove, rubbing palms together, we longed for space. We made up games and read books, but as the winter wore on and we felt we could bear it no more, we pulled on warm clothes and wandered outside in search of signs of thaw.

The tree out front, we discovered, leaked sugar water. We tapped into it with the sharp end of a nail, used a hammer to break into its flesh, then pressed our mouths to the rough bark and waited for the tree to bleed. It was slow in coming, but the taste was clean and cool and sweet. A few cars passed and drivers stared at the sight of children licking on trees. We ignored them. The sap fell onto our tongues and we had nowhere else to be, so we waited — mouths opened, latched onto the giant old maple.

36

Linny was Lana and Jolie's cousin. Sometimes she and her brother stayed at Billie's house. Her brother was tiny and wore a metal brace on his thin right leg. Both children had soft brown skin, short bowl cuts, and Asiatic eyes. They were delicate flowers, and quietly preferred by the adults.

One night, Linny dreamt of a gagohsa, and soon after there was a healing ceremony. Gagohsa was Seneca for ghost — a spirit who visited people in their dreams, and was chased away with smoke and rattles and chants. But best of all, his exit was celebrated with bread. Indeed, the only bread around for miles was reserved for ghosts.

From the moment Linny made her gagohsa announcement, I began to eye her. I wanted to know what she knew. As her healing began, I pressed my ear to the door and listened from the bedroom. I heard the shake of mud-turtle rattles, smelled the fire, watched as smoke swirled in from cracks in the door. Chants and ashes were blown over the girl, who emerged from her healing more serious than ever, a rough strap of leather tied to her wrist.

After Linny's healing, the women baked ghostbread.

It was fried into golden wheels in deep cast-iron skillets, or sizzled into hand-sized splatters of dough, or formed into puffy bricks and baked in the oven, only to be slathered with butter and sprinkled with sugar when it was taken out. Light on the tongue and heavy in the stomach, Ghostbread drove the taste of soup away, and was far better than any religion for convincing me of heaven.

As I threw myself into the bread's soft interior, I considered Linny and her gagohsa. I was intrigued by everything about the ceremony and considered staging a ghost-sighting myself, but decided against it, thinking that gagohsas probably paid no mind to palefaces anyway.

The Senecas made much of trees.

Spirits lived in the wood, they said, and could be captured in masks cut from living trees. The masks had mouths set in permanent scowls, and were meant to ward off gagohsas. Billie said that if the tree lived after the mask was taken, it brought good luck to its wearer.

At a powwow, I watched from afar as men in masks danced in an open field. I wandered. Whites were not allowed to enter the long house, and in truth, I had not even thought about entering that skeleton of saplings until the moment it was forbidden. I ate a hamburger from a food vendor and watched lacrosse players from other reservations.

Retracing my steps, I found Jolie and her mother sitting on a long slab of wood made into a bench. We swapped stories about what we'd seen. Then Billie, her long hair falling forward, pressed a stick into the ground and said, "Come on now, we better leave if we want to see the burning of the white dog."

Part of a ceremony the Senecas performed; the dog was burnt and sent as a messenger to the Great Spirit. "It cleans us," Billie said as she led us over to the field.

"I don't want to go," I said, and pulled away from the small crowd beginning to gather around the center of the field. Billie looked at me and laughed, her face wide and brown and friendly.

"It's just a part of the Handsome Lake religion," she said. I'd heard of Handsome Lake, but his name and religion were nothing I'd been able to make sense of.

"And the dog is fake, if you really have to know," she said, still smiling. "We wouldn't hurt any real dog." Billie turned and took Jolie's hand then and they headed toward a post that had been stuck into the ground with a small stuffed dog tied to its base.

"But why is the dog white?" I called after them, rubbing the pale skin of my wrist.

"Why is he white?" I asked again, but it was too late.

My question flailed behind Billie, and was taken up by the wind.

38

There was a hole in Billie's front yard.

The hole was actually the beginning of a basement that had been dug for a larger house back when Billie thought she could pay for such a thing. A few springs of rain and thaw had filled the hole with water, and by the time we arrived, it had become a regular feature of Billie's yard. A pond, almost. The water in the hole started out clean and woody as sap, but by August, it had lowered itself, and rusted-out bike frames and old tires broke through an algae-laden surface. Kids threw things into the hole, ran around it, stood close enough to feel the tug of danger, then backed off.

Most water came from a distribution center. We went once a week in pickups and cars to collect enough water for drinking, bathing, and cooking. Drinking water was kept just off the kitchen in a metal basin, where we used a silver ladle to drop it into our mouths. We bathed in the sink, Billie's sister using her long red nails to wash our scalps. She poured warm water over the backs of our heads, squeezed curlicues of cool shampoo onto crowns of wet hair, and scrubbed. We stood in a line and approached the sink one at a time, heads bowed.

39

In late summer, someone threw a party. Families came from other parts of Tonawanda and from as far away as the Allegany and Cattaraugus reservations. Kids ran wild and thirsty through the mowed sections of Billie's land. I lingered near the water basin, scooping cool water into my mouth while other kids yelled and screamed, caught up in their games. Feeling someone's eyes on me, I looked up. A girl. A stranger, nearly a teenager. She was smiling, and wore pink lipstick and a miniature plastic Pepsi bottle on a satin string around her neck.

When she saw me notice her, she headed my way. As she moved, the amber liquid in the bottle splashed inside its clear plastic container. The Pepsi necklace stopped my heart — it was the best thing I'd ever seen. I must have stared as she approached, for in an unexpected gesture of kindness, she removed it from her neck and circled it around mine.

I stood taller suddenly and followed her around all afternoon. When the older girls finally tsked-tsked my presence, she abandoned them and asked if I wanted to bike-ride. I said yes and grabbed the handlebars. I sat on the front half of the gold-flecked banana seat while her bronzed legs pushed at the pedals from the rear.

"Can you steer?" she asked, her voice a song.

I nodded the lie, convincing myself that steering didn't really matter and that riding worth anything was done in a straight line anyway — besides, I had no clue why this girl had befriended me and didn't want to spoil it all with something as unfortunate as the truth.

The ride was glorious. We breezed past groups of jump-roping girls, and I imagined myself a bird. A silver-winged bird. All of this, until we approached the hole. Straight ahead. Black-mouthed and ugly. I froze.

Other kids screamed, adults stood and looked our way, and my older friend asked again about my steering ability, her voice sounding suddenly alarmed. I had no answer as we plunged toward the late summer hole and only wondered what it would feel like to be swallowed by something so rank. I heard the vulgar croaking of bullfrogs, spied a rusted-out fender and calculated the exact place we'd land. I closed my eyes and prepared for our launch, the sound of kids screaming and the wind on my face somehow sharper as we flew at the hole.

Just then, she slammed her body to one side, stopped the bike with the tangle of her legs, and pushed us onto the hole's grassy edge. I looked down and realized I'd gotten away with only minor injuries. I waited for her anger. But it did not come. Instead she wiped dirt and grass from my lemon-yellow shorts, and when I tried to hand the necklace back, told me to keep wearing it.

I wore it for the rest of the afternoon and watched its liquid move as I jumped and ran, felt the solidity of it flapping against my halter top. My neck had never been so proud. When the party ended, she asked if I'd like to have it. And, though it was exquisite, the feel of it around my neck somehow anchoring me, I could not bring myself to receive it.

So once again I lied, and shook my head no.

40

Petey was the one to watch for.

He was big.

His fat brown fingers clutched at giant-sized bags of potato sticks, corn chips, cheese curls, or whatever other oversized portion of snack food had been on sale the day his mother went shopping. Though older than me and my sisters, Billie's baby brother was still a boy, the youngest of all her mother's sons. Even so, Petey strode around the place like an oily-fingered king.

We fashioned tall grasses into huts out in the field while Petey sat on an old stump, holding his snack food in one hand, while he fed himself with the other, eating and watching. On days when I had any pride at all, I ignored the fat boy and his greasy bag. But pride was a luxury not always afforded, and most days found me licking my lips and begging Petey for some chips. He wouldn't share — I knew this, but couldn't help myself and begged anyway. He beamed, loving the way I wanted what was his and his alone. It made him larger. He'd take out a chip, toss it onto his tongue, and then chew it, loud and sticky, his mouth open all the while.

Sometimes he even held the bag out to me. I knew the game, but approached anyway. Whenever he lifted his snacks high in the air, he'd watch as my arms flailed, and then push his lips into a tight, rippled "o," laughing his small circular laugh, his mouth like the tied end of an inflated pink balloon.

The only one he ever shared with was Steph. She was tough and quiet and could have snatched the bag right out of his hands if she had wanted. Petey seemed to admire her for her bravery, and so from time to time would extend his bag to her. Sometimes she'd grab a handful of cheese balls and split them with me, but usually her pride was larger than he was and she steered clear of the big boy and his bag of snacks altogether.

I wondered at her strength, almost glad that it wasn't me he liked; for I knew just how easily I'd have been swayed, slipped my hand into his bag, and stood at his side, his greasy queen, helping rule over a yard full of hungry kids.

41

Someone's father showed up one day, in jeans and soiled leather boots. He walked into Billie's house like he'd always belonged, legs stretched out, cigarette dangling from his fingers. He'd brought three Marathon candy bars with him. Marathon bars were long chocolate and caramel braids advertised on TV to go "on and on," and I wanted one of those endless bars of candy more than anything. I lay on my belly and stared at the man as he visited with his woman's children. I was not above making my eyes pitiful as he unwrapped the chocolate. In fact, I made them as pitiful as possible and directed them at the man whose hands were so red-brown they looked as though they'd been dipped in cherry varnish.

Fathers were a mystery to me — as arbitrarily assigned as the candy that was in front of my face. Who had one and who did not seemed little more than luck, so I told myself I hardly cared that I had no father to speak of. Still, I wanted that chocolate caramel braid and found myself wondering about the touch of those cherry-brown hands.

42

It seems to me that my family packed up and left on the very same day that Billie's mother came to the house, avoided everyone's eyes, and made her sour announcement.

"The welfare knows you're here," she said to no one in particular, but somehow indicating us. The words themselves made no sense to me, but I somehow understood that we were being told to leave. Certainly her words were strong enough to make my mother fly out the door.

She took her rage out on a field of weeds near the house, flinging any belongings that wouldn't fit in the car — photos, papers, her yellow-stained wedding dress — and leaving them heaped up in angry piles between milkweed and goldenrod. I didn't understand until much later about my mother's factory income counting against Billie and her kids, about the tribal council's righteous discomfort with the stream of white faces running through their land, how my baby sister's father was hardly ever around, or how his few comings and goings included a certain redhead who drove my mother crazy.

In the same way it seemed that mere hours elapsed between the old woman's announcement and our leaving, it also seemed suddenly clear that she had never liked my mother. I decided that the unsmiling face was worse than a gagohsa, and helped load up the Buick. We packed the car with whatever boxes and bags would fit, and my mother stopped at Bell's Market to buy food for the motel room that would house us for the days and nights to come. Bread and cheese.

I squished a slice of bread between my fingers, kneaded it into a pasty ball, and shoved it whole into my mouth.

43

My mother was crazy for birds.

That she was in love with all things winged was perhaps the most solid thing to be said about her. The rounded sweep of her cheek, the shy upturn of her smile — even the steel blue of her irises — none of these was clearer to me than her fondness for creatures of the sky. Perhaps because she was as migratory in nature as they were, my mother liked nothing better than to tilt her head upward and trace the departure of birds with her eyes. When a flock of geese passed overhead, she called us out to the yard, thrilled by their honking, told us to crane our necks and follow their movement through the clouds.

"Hurry kids! Come on now, or you'll miss them."

This mother who pulled gnarled vegetables from pockets of stubborn earth and made them into something soft and warm, who laughed off things like sassy children and hairy-legged spiders, who maneuvered lightly through all manner of political and religious conversation — saying her part, but listening, too — this same woman sounded frantic while calling us out to see birds. Failing to set our eyes upon a flock in flight was a sin of omission to her, and there was more worry in her voice over missing out on a bird or two than when she wondered aloud how to pay the rent.

It was like a parade to her, all that commotion on high. She couldn't get enough of the trumpeting, the beating of wings, the buzz of flight. And if whatever yard or porch we inhabited did not offer a big enough view, she'd drive out to the wildlife refuge for a better look at mallards, tundra swans, and snow geese.

She went there often — to savor a good mood, or to quell a low one. She loved the sanctuary and could spend whole afternoons tracking the take-off and landing of birds. She knew the land, all its plants and animals, its strangled bodies of water. It was hers, like a child — or better, perhaps, because it asked nothing in return.

Convincing herself that we loved it, too, she herded us into the car, and made her drives to the refuge a form of family recreation. We complained, but she'd pack us into the car just the same, tell us to stop our whining, for heaven's sake, and try to find something pretty to look at.

And why should a bird sanctuary be the place my mother most liked to visit? Better than a trip to the cool brick rooms of the Swan Library, better than the luxury of resting among strangers over a cup of coffee at the diner on Main Street, better even than sitting sloppy and happy in a kitchen full of talkative cousins?

Perhaps she was able to find peace there. With all that silence and sky, perhaps she was able to travel to places far away. Or maybe the refuge, with its unspoiled land, reminded her of home — her first home, the one her father had built from trees growing at the base of granite mountains.

She talked about him often, her father. He was the only man she ever spoke of without salt on her tongue. To her (and to us, who never knew him) he was a giant of a man, a sort of saint really, and everything the long-dead were supposed to be. Quiet and good-hearted. Solid and hardworking. Honest. She had nothing but love for her father, the woodsman who had learned the art of storytelling as a boy sitting around the logging camps of northern Maine, the copper-haired Swede with a cleft in his chin, whose worn hands carried home bags of sweets for his middle child and only daughter.

The Iroquois Wildlife Refuge stood just east of Buffalo, between the Tonawanda Indian Reservation and Albion, north of Batavia and the factory job my mother held. Indeed, that was how she first found the place, on break one day from the metal-walled rooms. Though we'd abandoned the big old house in Albion, and had left behind the tiger lilies and bullfrogs of the reservation, we'd still file out of the motel room that housed us and load ourselves into the car for a drive past Old Orchard Creek, into the freshwater marshes and hardwood swamps. We complained, of course, as we pressed faces and knees into the tight compartment of the car, but in truth, we'd been trailing our mother for years and knew nothing else. For the past four years in fact, those sodden acres and their winged residents had been about the most consistent feature in our lives, more regular than the clothes we wore, the schools we attended, the beds or floors or chairs we slept on.

And so my mother brushed aside our grumbling as she would have a passing swarm of gnats, hands in the air, batting back the dark-eyed glances and snotty remarks launched at her through the rearview mirror.

"You kids just don't know how to have a good time," she'd say, seeming hurt and genuinely perplexed by our lack of enthusiasm. She must have wondered how such a sad and heavy defect could have taken hold of anything that had come from her. Her mood always lightened, though, as she steered the car onto the marshy refuge road, her lightness becoming excitement as we passed thistle and cattail and finally pulled into the lot where she parked and headed down to the pond, banged-up binoculars in hand.

Some of us followed my mother down the trail, but a few stayed behind and kicked our feet through gravel while leaning against the car, swatting insects from our hair, and complaining about how hot it was.

"How long you gonna be anyway?" someone always asked.

And though she'd be halfway to the pond by then, she'd turn back, glance over her shoulder, and catch our eyes long enough to put a finger to her lips and shush us.

"You'll scare the birds away," she'd say, and make her descent to the milky pond below.

44

He was a proud man, her father.

Maybe too proud, though she'd never say such a thing. After years in the wilds of northern Maine, he found himself a wife and headed west, to New Hampshire. She was fierce and young, a dark-haired girl whose beauty was more chiseled than soft, whose people were said to be Mohawk. She married the thick-fingered man to escape an arthritic mother, a stranger of a stepfather, and a choking brood of brothers and sisters. She traded them in for just one man. It must have been an easy exchange.

She cooked and cleaned, canned and sewed, gave him two sons and a daughter. He cut down trees and she cooked pies, and the world remained that way for nearly two decades. Until he fell sick. He worked until he couldn't, refused to see a doctor, refused to allow his wife to take a job, refused to let the family accept the boxes of food and pile of army blankets offered them by kind-hearted neighbors.

His young daughter spent those nights shivering in bed, listening as her father, hero and saint, moaned in pain from the room next door. That was the way things were. Frozen. No one shutting an eye, barely a whisper between them.

Until his young wife had had enough. She defied her husband, found a job cleaning rooms at an inn, put food on the table. And though his pride was damaged at having a woman support him, things seemed for a time as though they might be improving.

The real trouble came when my mother's mother learned to drive. She was good at it. She loved the feel of the wheel in her hands, and once she'd grabbed hold of it — this young wife and mother who had not been softened by children, who had no outlet for her energies other than cooking and sewing, whose longing must have felt like bits of wool flowering under the skin — once she was able to drive, she bought a car, and spent more time in its hold than anywhere else. Freedom. A new taste in her mouth, hot and persuasive. The click of the key in the ignition, the rush of air tumbling through rolled-down windows, the spray of dirt under the tires, the hushed voice of Johnny Mathis singing directly into her ear — this was everything. The air loosened around her. And for the first time in her life, my grandmother began to breathe.

45

"Who could really blame her?" my mother would ask of her mother when she came to that part of the story, her voice betraying the answer.

"She was young and pretty and didn't like being cooped up in a kitchen." Her words must have felt something like charity, and I wondered at how hard things must have been for my mother as a girl.

And then there was the ending, the sad truth of the matter, the part of the story most often set aside in the telling: My grandmother left her husband, proud as a rock, sick and dying, alone in a bed near the foot of the White Mountains. She packed up her clothes and her children, pushed them into the car, and never looked back.

"That's the last time I ever saw my father," my mother would say, then clam right up. I imagined her longing for another hour with him, could see the way she wished her mother had driven away without her. Her father, the mountain, that place — all were lost to her. And because my mother did not grieve, they became her fairytales, the stories she returned to over and over, the paths she most often walked upon.

They traveled. Her mother and her siblings. A few streets away. A few towns away. A few states away. Finally landing at the family's farm near Lake Champlain in New York State. The visit was a good one, people talked and ate and laughed. Big stories were told, bigger plans were made. But the freedom so recently found was honey on my grandmother's tongue, and even as she wiped tears of laughter from her eyes, she kept those car keys in hand. In the end, the temptation of all those roads leading west would not let her be.

"I'll be back in no time," said my mother's once-contained, now wild-eyed momma, keys jangling between thumb and forefinger. "Wait here, I'll be back in a week," said the woman, who might have had the best intentions, but would not return for over a year.

After a few weeks of cousins gossiping about where she'd gone to, my grandmother's children were scared and shamed. When they realized she wasn't coming back, the two boys took off and somehow made their way east, back over two state lines. Only my mother did as she was told and waited, withstanding the bewildered looks and muttering of cousins. She worked at the family farm and restaurant to earn her keep, rising early each morning to milk cows and set tables before heading off to high school.

46

We'd sometimes set out on our own, walk the trails, tiptoe over rackety bridges, looking for tadpoles in shallow pools. Other times we followed our mother, listening as she told her stories and pointed out wildflowers. Mayapple. Queen Anne's lace. Trout lily. We watched her watching the sky, delighted in her delight when a heron set off — the majesty of its slender body, still as a reed, stretching itself into flight. She kept her eyes on the gray-blue bird as it made its way up and over our heads, followed the gigantic flap, swish, and glide. Once the heron had passed overhead and landed in some far-off tree, she'd look at us, her face pink with joy.

"There," she'd say, "did you see that?" a bit of the sky in her voice.

As though it were magic. As though a heron in flight didn't happen every time we came. Of course we saw it — and of course we loved it — but we were knots of children, cruel in our love for her, and this bit of kindness we could not give, asking instead, yet again, when we could leave.

"Not yet," she would say, and then look into our faces, taking pains to remind herself that she was the mother, trying to sound the part, though the look of the child inevitably slipped through the eyes, and there was a plea there, too.

"Not yet," she'd whisper. "Let's find just one more."

47

I sat on the bed and stared at the side-by-side boxes of Cheerios and powdered milk perched atop a pressed-wood dresser. The two boxes were the same size and dimensions, and while I loathed the taste of dried milk mixed with lukewarm water, those boxes still managed to seem like treats.

We were in a motel just off the New York State Thruway. Our room was one of eight that sat in a strip along the parking lot. Dented aluminum chairs painted aqua and white were scattered on the narrow walkway between rooms and cars. We'd be living there until my mother found us a permanent place.

She worked and we went to school, and afterward, we crammed into the room, where I watched TV or closed my eyes and tried to be alone with my thoughts.

I replayed the clips of our most recent departure in my head, pictured my mother flinging her black storage trunk and its contents into a field on the day we left, remembered how no one dared approach her as she tossed years of photographs, legal papers, and our much prized cookie jar into tall grass and weeds. I recalled how we watched and waited by the doors of the green car that whisked us off the reservation and to the motel.

Once I'd spun those memories around my head until they made me dizzy from too much handling, I moved on to other matters.

Like where we were headed next.

I tried to imagine living here long-term, tried to picture what life might be like in this room, everyone fighting over who'd get the bed, who'd get the fold-out chair, who would simply be left the floor.

I thought about the pile of white towels brought to our room each day and where they came from and how many towels the owners could have and what a miracle their constant replenishment seemed.

I thought about how warm water felt on my skin, and how pretty the sight of suds winding their way down a drain could be.

But here's what I thought of most.

This was my secret:

I could control the wind.

Like Isis, the TV goddess, who carried a crow on her shoulder, wore a white silk tunic, and could conjure the wind when the mood struck.

I loved Isis.

I couldn't get over how she started out like everyone else, just a regular girl who became a goddess by holding on to an amulet and calling out to the wind.

And how she flew! She lifted off the ground with the force of her will and a simple incantation: "Zephyr winds which blow on high, lift me now so I may fly."

Just an everyday girl till she pushed herself up and floated among the clouds.

I closed my eyes and imagined a silky tunic falling over my body, a crow cawing from my shoulder. I pushed my arms behind my back, thrust my body forward, called out to the wind and opened my eyes to find leaves jingling like strings of chimes.

I could feel myself rising, hovering, brushing against the tops of trees.

That's what I did while I waited in that room: I conjured the wind. I shook the trees.

I didn't know how I did it, and if I ever told anyone — Steph or my mother — they'd have laughed. So I kept it to myself, and brought it out only while lying there, considering cereal boxes and the warmth of running water. I kept the secret in my pocket, and sometimes, when things were just right, I'd let myself feel the wind swelling at the bottoms of my feet.

48

"Come on, kids," my mother said one day after a long shift at the gypsum factory, "pack up your stuff."

She walked into the room, dropped her keys on the bedside table, then headed to the sink to wipe the white powder from her hands.

"Come on now," she called from the bathroom, "let's get ready to leave."

Just like that.

Just when I'd begun to get used to the ease of motel-room living, we were leaving. I'd grown attached to the stiffly laundered towels, the cool tile floor clean against my feet, the magic of indoor plumbing. But we were moving, my mother said, tomorrow after school.

This time we were headed east, back to Rochester.

"You were born here," my mother said as our car exited the New York State Thruway and we headed north, to the city's core. "We've lived in this city before."

I pressed my face against the glass of our overwrought car as it pulled down Grand Avenue and parked in front of number seventy-eight. I remembered bits of the city, of course, and we'd had visits, but I'd never noticed how close together the houses were, how they seemed to lean on each other for support.

I sat there, and though my body somehow stretched into its new surroundings, a part of me never really unfolded myself from that car. A part of me stayed there, cheek pressed against glass, trying to take it all in.

49

Charlie was the color of chocolate milk. His creamy brown skin was only odd when you considered the fact that his parents were whiter than bleached and bromated flour. Charlie, they said, had a rare blood disease. The blood disease had bronzed Charlie's skin and coiled his hair into tight black springs. It was not until later that I began to doubt the blood disease story. Not until ninth-grade science class, learning about dominant traits and alleles, that I thought about Charlie, his alleles, and recalled the man with a toothy smile and flame-tipped dashiki who stuffed a black fisted Afro pick into the back pocket of skin-tight jeans while hanging around on Charlie's front porch, talking to Marlene.

Marlene, Charlie's mom, went by "Mar," and while she might not have known much about dominant traits and alleles, Mar understood how much easier it was to catch a tight-jeaned man than a rare blood disease.

A curvy version of Natasha from the Rocky and Bullwinkle show, Mar took long drags from her cigarette and tossed smooth streams of smoke over her shoulder. She went shoeless most days and the bottoms of her feet were black except for the crescent-shaped undersides of her arches. She melted vanilla ice cream on her tongue and kissed it into the mouths of the babies she cared for. I wanted to turn away from her on account of the filthy feet and her birdlike feeding of the young, but couldn't. The pout of her lower lip, the slant of the long-lashed eyes, the way she offered no explanation as she blew her smoke and mashed up baby meals in her mouth — these things kept me watching.

Dwayne was Mar's man, Charlie's identified daddy. And on those rare occasions when they were not filled with brown-bagged bottles of wine, his long fingers cupped Mar's ass. Sometimes he held the wine in one hand, the ass in the other. His world, united.

Dwayne loved Charlie. Despite the blood disease, or perhaps because of it, Charlie was his golden boy. He loved Mar, too, judging by the fact that he lived with her. But this was Dwayne, not some TV dad, so despite his affection for Mar, he kept a wife and seven children three streets over. In fact, Mar had been the babysitter until Dwayne could no longer limit his urges to rushed encounters here and there and simply ditched his wife for the pulpy-lipped girl. The ditching of his wife, however, amounted to no more than an address change, and in reality, Dwayne somehow managed to stretch his fingers around the asses of both women.

Charlie's family lived in the house behind us. My mother had known Mar for years, and it had been Mar, in fact, who helped her find the half-house for rent on Grand Avenue.

Mar had other children, besides the gold-skinned Charlie. Before Charlie. Before the tight-jeaned man. Before Dwayne. When she was still a girl. There were three of them, two boys who were practically men, and a daughter who at fifteen, by neighborhood standards, was more woman than girl. Sheri was sour, and spent all her time dreaming up the wedding she'd have some day, the sparkling white church, the waterfall of flowers, the impossibly ruffled dresses. She tried to pull off smoking like her mother, who, despite her dirt-encrusted feet, was prettier than Sheri would ever be.

Sheri loved James, Dwayne's boy from his other woman, but for some reason, their love was not allowed. The vaguely incestuous nature of the arrangement seemed less of a concern than the fact that Dwayne was the head of both households and wanted to keep things straight. Plus Sheri said that Dwayne came into her room some nights and tried to talk his drunken way into her panties, so maybe he simply didn't want his son going into territory he had planned for himself.

James was long-limbed and dark-haired. He went around without a shirt, showing off fine round shoulders and a hard belly that slid clean into loose-fitting cut-offs. He was as lovely as Sheri was plain.

They sometimes paid me quarters to play look out. I got twenty-five cents for every fifteen minutes of standing at the edge of the front yard, looking both ways, and calling out when Dwayne was spotted. I was not to look in their direction while Sheri and the dark-haired boy fell into the cool opening of the front hall. My job was simply to shout when I saw Dwayne rounding the corner. Otherwise, I left them alone and collected quarters.

I learned two things from Sheri.

First, my legs were too thick to wear boys' basketball socks anymore. "Those orange and black stripes make your calves look big," she said, "stick to sandals."

Second, I was smart.

I overheard this while Steph and I were sitting on the dull hardwood of our living room floor, tracing invisible patterns with our fingers. The front door was open and older people had gathered down on the porch. Someone was talking about how smart Stephanie was. This was nothing new; everyone knew Steph was smart. At ten, my sister scavenged parts from lawn mowers and fashioned them into go-carts. She searched sale flyers, made shopping lists, and tried to persuade my mother to budget. She could find her way to sections of the city I'd never even heard of. Clearly, she was bright. And whenever there was a lull in the conversation, or space that needed filling, people talked about how smart Steph was instead of the weather or what the president was doing.

But this time was different.

Sheri interrupted and said that I was smart, too, according to the school.

My head snapped up.

Steph stared hard at the floor, pushed her finger along the space between the shellacked wood planks, and pretended not to hear. I was smart. I didn't know what Sheri meant exactly, but glommed onto it nonetheless.

I liked being smart for about three days.

Until, in school, Mrs. Santarocco told the class that I'd scored high on the California Achievement Test. She asked me to stand. I turned red. I had just begun to fade into the background after our midyear transfer when she walked over with a package in her hands, something special for the high scorer. Some sort of plant. A baby tree. She stretched it out to me and then, just as I lifted my arm to take the sapling, she pulled back.

She'd just remembered, she said, about our being renters, and was not sure whether renters could plant trees. She pursed her lips and surveyed the class with puckered eyes, as if third graders might have access to such information. She'd have to check, she said, then turned away and deposited the sapling into the classroom sink, where I looked at its frilled head from time to time. The roots and trunk were bound in plastic and beads of moisture formed on the clear wrap as the day wore on, so that by the end of the day, you could hardly make out the green inside.

50

I learned a few new words on my first day at School no. 11: honkie, Oreo, blow job. A honkie was a white person, my mother said, and blow job was a dirty word for something adults did. She didn't know anything about Oreos, but I soon learned that they were kids with one black parent and one white parent. Honkies could also be called crackers, and someone who was an Oreo only minutes before could safely be referred to as a zebra when the mood struck.

Color was important on Grand Avenue. We all wore shoes fished from discount bins and received free lunch, so what else was there?

51

Rufus and Jewel lived in the apartment beneath ours. Jewel was tall and thin with skin the color of creamed coffee. Easily the prettiest woman on the street, she walked with a straight back and had once been a catalog model. Pages from Sears and Kmart ads were displayed in the built-in bookcase of their living room: Jewel in active wear; Jewel in evening wear; Jewel in underwear. A dark-skinned Barbie, she was just about perfect, on catalog pages and in life, until she smiled to reveal a gold-capped front tooth.

Everything in their half of the house shined. The sofa was copper and gold velour, the tables were smoked glass, the air smelled of cocoa butter and marijuana. I baby-sat for Jewel's one-year-old son and she paid me in gifts of purses, perfume, and Avon holiday edition soaps.

Jewel's baby was fat and bronze and had a sloppy wet smile. My baby sister was about the same age but so well-loved that by the time I got hold of her, Rachel had tired of cooing. Jewel's baby, on the other hand, giggled and drooled, ate up the attention. And so while Rufus and Jewel went out dancing, I held on to his warm flesh while running my hands along cool glass tabletops.

52

My bed was in the living room. So was Steph's. I'd spent years sleeping on floors, of course, and so didn't know enough to care about sleeping in the living room. All I knew was that suddenly we had beds, and as Steph attempted to divide up the living room with cardboard boxes and crates carried up from the street, I became mesmerized by my sheets. I flapped a worn one with floral edging into the air over my bed and let it fall onto the mattress. Over and over. I loved the bubble of air that formed under the clean cotton. I had a crush on that bed, thinking of it when I was not near it, slipping into its protection whenever I could.

53

Despite her wishes to the contrary, Stephanie was pretty. Waist-length hair hung like a thundercloud around a full mouth and cola-colored eyes. She was tiny, and could have been a doll had she been so inclined, but beauty was an unimportant variable to her, a hindrance, if anything — much like being a girl in the first place. She wouldn't allow anyone to comb her tangle of hair, and howled the time mother told her she was getting too old to go around shirtless. Her favorite outfit was a pair of pants with leopards running wild, up and down the length of each leg. And a matching safari vest. She loved the sleek and handsome James West from *Wild, Wild West* with his black bolo hat and quiet confidence, and talked often about how fun it would be to shimmy up gutters and jump from rooftops.

She was a tomboy. I heard people say it, and took note of the admiration hanging in their voices. Hoping some of it might rub off, I followed her around. But it was Steph, not I, who jumped from two-story porches, did chin-ups ten at a time, fought anyone, anytime — even boys. And it was into her ear, not mine, that Terrence let his secrets fall.

Though he was in her grade at school, Terrence was older than Steph. Eleven or twelve. Tough and quiet, his mother was a hooker whose skin shone with makeup and perspiration. Her doorways sparkled with long strands of plastic beads; red velvet pillows lined a leather sofa.

Based on the nature of his mother's work, Terrence was not allowed to play inside, and when he was out on his porch, he was selective of his friends. Steph was one of the few he invited to join him as he hopped fences, cut through back alleyways, and explored neighborhoods beyond our own.

I was tight with self-pity, couldn't stand their adventures, couldn't stand the way Steph began to mimic Terrence, the way she'd taken to saying "finsta" for "fixing to." Finsta this and finsta that. She and Terrence were always finsta do something.

Though generally levelheaded, Steph thought nothing of making her hands into fists and fighting. Boys her age and older feared her. Rice lived on Grand, had squinty eyes, and called himself "the San Francisco treat." As if his self-imposed nickname weren't enough to mark him, he made the mistake of engaging Stephanie in combat. He'd run up, touch her, or say something whenever he passed. Rice must have been stupid, or simply desperate for attention. No matter. Steph would tackle him, pin his shoulders under her knees, and stuff his shirt with freshly mown grass.

"Let me up, let me up," he'd cry, his voice ragged. He would whine and beg and threaten to call the police while we all gathered round, laughing. We hated Rice. For his weakness. His lack of judgment. His mewling. He was always out of school healing from car accidents that people said his mother made him have for the insurance money.

"Why don't you stop your crying and go jump in front of a car," we'd say when Steph finally released him. And he'd run home, grass falling from his sleeves, calling over his shoulder about getting the law involved.

54

Like flowers in the desert that somehow manage without water, religion flourished on Grand Avenue. A Bible-Baptist couple one block over provided theological instruction in their backyard. They paid in candy for those who brought other kids to them. They gave Bibles, stickers, and Tootsie Rolls to anyone able to memorize and recite the words to John 3:16:

"For God so loved the world, that he gave his only begotten Son, that whosoever believeth in him should not perish, but have everlasting life."

I went a few times, memorized and recited the passage to earn the Bible, the candy, their easy admiration. They were nice, though their good manners and concern for my eternal soul seemed out of place in the neighborhood. Still, I liked to read and eat sweets, and so attended their backyard lessons as often as I could, my fervor only dying as their candy supply dwindled.

A Pentecostal church three houses down held services in Spanish, which didn't stop our mother from herding us there once a week. We'd been baptized Catholic, but it didn't matter. The church on Grand Avenue could have spoken in tongues and handled snakes and she wouldn't have cared. She was still commuting to her job near the refuge and stopping on break to see herons. She was high and light and prone to flights of fancy, and thought the church would be a good idea.

"It's so pretty inside with all those windows," she said, and added, "Maybe we'll learn some Spanish."

Everyone smiled and sang, and we made friends with the Padilla family, who lived next door to the church, whose father wore starched shirts and ties, and whose mother invited us girls to learn to embroider hand towels. With two parents, a house they actually owned, and a fence that circled their front and back yards, closing off their property to the rest of the street, the Padillas were the elite of our neighborhood. Because the Padilla kids were our age and because their parents thought we were somehow different from the other grubby kids on Grand, they allowed us to unlatch the front gate and join them.

On Sundays, after attending the church service we didn't understand, we visited the Padillas, played kickball, and ate the greasy foods their mother served. Arroz con gandules. Bacalao. Platanos fritos. We loved playing in their deep green yard, instead of in the street, where we had to stop our game every few minutes to let cars pass. The oldest Padilla girl liked my brother Anthony. His long hair and her flirting with him in see-through pink cotton shirts somehow went unnoticed by Mr. Padilla, and our way of life became almost routine.

Until I fought with Itza.

Itza was my age, and must have said something mean about my being white or having mismatched clothes, so I said something back and we fought. Behind the church. The lawn was in need of mowing; we were alone in grass that went to our knees. Everyone else was in church, their thin singing leaking out the windows. Having always relied on Steph to do my fighting, I didn't even know where to begin.

It was awkward for that first moment, the intimacy of standing face to face, the tension of the impending fight heavy in the air, my not knowing which hand or leg to push first into combat. Finally, when I realized I had to begin somehow or else stand fixed in starting pose forever, I grabbed hold of the gold hoop hanging from Itza's right ear and yanked it down. Hard.

She held her ear and screamed. There was blood on her finger and she cried out so loudly I covered my ears until her crying beat out the singing, and people came running, looking at me with disdain.

Que mala esa blanca — what a bad white girl.

Mrs. Padilla wiped Itza's ear with one of her embroidered washcloths while my mother swiped me in the head and apologized for my behavior.

"I understand," Mrs. Padilla said. "Kids will be kids."

But after our fight, the Padilla gates closed to us and we stopped attending the church where none of us ever knew what was being said anyway.

55

My mother's car broke down and changed everything. Unable to afford the repairs, she could no longer make the hour-long commute to Batavia for her factory job, and the green Buick became just one more stopped car in the wide driveway that separated us from the three-tiered apartment building next door. With the car dead, we were as stuck as everyone else.

Caseworkers appeared in our kitchen from the Department of Social Services, asking lists of questions that my mother answered in a hushed voice. She swatted us away as she spoke, but when I heard the social worker ask questions about fathers, I strained to hear. Except for the oldest three kids, none of us even knew our fathers, and the very word, used in our house, was enough to cause silence. My mother's voice became quieter with each question, until she eventually refused to answer.

In the end, I learned nothing, but we began to receive rainbow-colored money for food. Meanwhile, my mother started a series of lower-paying jobs and the perpetual search for something better — a job with more pay, fewer hours, less strenuous work.

I had never seen my mother's spirits so low. Her mood sagged, and she spent any time away from work in bed. Like a bird with a broken wing, she circled quietly around us, and became hard to look at.

We began to fight.

Our living space had been more modern at the motel, but on Grand, for the first time in years, all of us were under one roof. Counting my baby sister, there were seven kids now — all growing, all clawing for space.

The bird sanctuary was out of reach. There were no gravel roads to walk up and down until we were worn out, no fields to sprawl out into, no giant birds or hiking trails to lighten moods. On Grand Avenue, whether we walked east or west, everything looked the same. Neighborhood men bubbled on porches, and even the youngest of boys pushed their legs into pimp walks, and forced their mouths into tough talk.

Lisa took to wearing a light blue T-shirt with the word BITCH spelled out in sparkly letters. The glittery word stretched the width of her shirt and expanded gradually and in direct proportion to the development of her bust. Lisa wore that BITCH shirt like a badge. She was surly, talked back to my mother, and once, after getting slapped for something she'd said, Lisa hit back. My mother's mouth hung open. Lisa hit again. My mother grabbed a broom and tried to hold Lisa back. Though only ninety pounds, Lisa was tight as a fist. Both were red in the face, unwilling to give. Lisa was all backbone and pushing forward. And my mother, for her part, was stunned and trying to hold onto something she'd already lost.

The rest of us girls cried. No one had ever hit my mother. Everything seemed changed. Broken. We knew Lisa's anger and my mother's stubborn pride and were sure it would end in death.

We screamed for them to stop, and when neither listened, Steph shepherded us into the bathroom where she sat us on towels she'd rolled into cushions and told us it would be okay. We bit our lips and tried to block out the sounds of fighting while she ran to the kitchen and came back with cans of creamed corn and wax beans.

"Don't worry," she said to our bent heads, taking time to look into each of our faces, "we'll stay in this bathroom for as long as we need to, even live here if we have to."

56

She must have felt it happening.

The way she couldn't keep us in line anymore.

My mother did what she could, even designed and implemented a behavior modification program. She used poster board and felt-tip markers to create a chart with columns and rows, said she wanted us to share in the housework. Things were different now, she said, and she needed our help. Washing dishes. Sweeping floors. Scrubbing the bathtub. Next to each name was a list of tasks and corresponding rewards. She took great care in drawing the lines and explaining the rules. We earned points for doing a job. We traded points for treats. But after a few days of working to earn the same hot chocolate packets and cookies we got for free at Mar's house, we abandoned our chores, and the chart became a silly flag flapping on the inside of the kitchen cabinet.

57

In late January, snow whipped in from Canada, gathered strength over Lake Ontario, and landed like a hard and heavy hand on western New York.

A blizzard.

One that people would talk about twenty years later. Snow covered the city with a blanket so thick, people couldn't move, and the schools had no choice but to release early. I forgot my mittens, or never had any to begin with, and kept my hands stuffed in my pockets and eyes lowered to the ground to minimize the impact of the wind. I pushed through snowdrifts more than half my height as a group of neighborhood kids walked home. They were excited by the blizzard, happy the schools had closed. All I could think was that my birthday was the next day, and I'd miss the balloon the teacher tied to each child's desk on her birthday. I had managed my envy over the last few balloons only by counting the days till I'd turn ten and have one of my own. And now I'd miss it.

Then I saw it.

Sifting in and out of snowdrifts in slow powdered swirls, the money seemed more dream than reality. A ten, some fives, and a few ones were covered and uncovered by snow as I watched. I called out to the other kids, but the wind was crazy and snow was everywhere and no one heard. I removed a hand from my pocket and reached into the snow, but my fingers were frozen and any bills I managed to get hold of slipped from the hook of my numb hand.

My brothers and sisters had moved on and one of them was turning back, yelling for me to come on. I tried to take hold of the money, but the more I grabbed, the more it fell back into the snow.

"Hey," someone called, "we have to go."

I settled for one final dip, came up with a few bills, and shoved the frozen clump of hand, money, and snow into my coat.

When we got home, I told everyone about the money and pushed into my pocket for the evidence. I dug deep into the orange lining of my parka but came up empty-handed. I dug. Further and further, each time producing nothing but snow. No one believed. They laughed while I blew on my hands and tried to remember the exact spot to return to when things thawed out.

58

Corpus Christi was our church. Despite our forays into the Pentacostal church on Grand and visits to the Bible-Baptists' backyard for candy and praise, Corpus was the Catholic church we'd attended for years. The place my mother had worshipped saints while practicing free love before leaving the city; the old brick building on the corner of Main and Prince where each of us had been baptized.

Someone from the church found out we were back in town, poorer than ever, and the parishioners swelled with generosity. They organized and collected, and a few days before Christmas, a nun with a raw face delivered two green garbage bags full of gifts. Steph and I watched as she and a helper lugged the bags upstairs, but hid as the front door was opened. We wanted the gifts, but couldn't bear the pity. We listened from another room, emerging only as we heard our mother thanking the givers one final time.

"Are you sure you wouldn't like cocoa?" she said, and when they refused, "Well, thank you," and "Merry Christmas," no trace of shame in her voice.

Steph and I came out from hiding to find that our mother had locked the bags away in the closet where she stored private things. The closet was in the living room, and took on a new power once the donated gifts were stashed inside.

Unable to resist the closet's mystique, we took to playing with the lock as we talked. We'd sit on the floor, fingers on the lock, turning it back and forth as we laughed and exchanged stories. We sat there for hours, twirling that lock like a strand of hair.

When we were alone, we tried to pick it. With hairpins, clothes hangers, the caps of pens. Nothing worked. Until I pried the thin silver key from a can of donated Spam and rushed it over to Steph, hoping she'd be impressed, but she only looked at me flat-lipped and said she didn't think it would work. Still, she took the tiny key into her hand, and when she tried it, the lock popped open.

The Spam key was a rare success for me, but I checked my loopy smile. I needed Steph, after all, more than I needed triumph, so I tucked my pride away and congratulated her on opening the door.

Inside, we found the bags of donated gifts along with the items our mother had managed to purchase on layaway — an assortment of things we had asked for and things others imagined poor children might like. Pushing through the gifts, we tried to decide who would get what. Rachel was the baby, so naturally she'd get the Gloworm. Will would get the tube socks; Anthony, the puzzle; Lisa, the perfumed lotion; and either of us could get the package marked "Girl, Aged 9-12."

59

My mother stopped cooking most days, and meal planning became beside the point. She wasn't around, and even when she was, she'd lost interest. Not counting holidays — when large feasts were prepared, the table set, and prayers read — we were essentially scavengers when it came to food.

Except when my mother baked.

Making something rise from flour seemed a comfort to her. She pushed thick strands of auburn hair into a rolled bandana and used her freckled hands to fashion cakes, cream puffs, and biscuits. Sifter and rolling pin in hand, my mother came alive as the air around her sweetened a bit.

There was a record player in the kitchen and my mother gave Anthony money to go to Record Theatre and buy Mallory a few 45s for her birthday. But he chose all wrong. My mother had wanted "Purple-People Eater" but Tony brought back Paul Simon and the Bay City Rollers for a five-year-old girl. Though disappointed, my mother said nothing and it became the thing to do to listen to Paul Simon go on about slip slidin' away while she steamed up the windows with her baking.

60

She stopped kissing me on Grand Avenue. My mother. At my request. Her leaning over each night and planting a kiss on my cheek began to feel weird. She sensed it, too, saw the way I wiggled and moved and thought of questions to distract her as she approached, so I knew she was thinking of me and not herself when she teased that I might be getting too big for goodnight kisses. I agreed, but was not prepared for the loss that often accompanies the truth. Nor did I expect the hollow flowering in my chest as I heard her make the goodnight rounds, kissing the others, those who still let her.

61

"Shoot me. Shoot me. Shoot meeeee!" I screamed over and over, loud as I could, till someone made a finger into a gun, used a mouth for sound effect, and launched bullets into the air.

"Puh, puh, puh, puh."

The sound of bullets whizzed my way. I raised my wrists to meet them, deflected them soundly with my tin-foil bands. Wonder Woman wore bands made of Feminum, a magic metal mined only on Paradise Island. But the coconut-scented place and its ore-producing Amazons were a long way from Grand Avenue, so the best I could do was to steal strips of aluminum foil from the kitchen and fold them into wide silver bracelets. I slapped them on my wrists and walked out the door, ready to face anyone, anywhere.

Sometimes the shooter would get fancy and use a machine gun, or two kids would come at me from different directions and shoot me at the same time — so that I had to separate my arms and keep both wrists in perpetual motion to meet the onslaught of air bullets.

But always, I managed.

I'd keep the wristbands on all day. I grabbed a bit of clothesline and coiled it into a loop at my waist. Steph sprayed my lasso gold with leftover bike paint. She was the only one who allowed me to use it on her, which is no great surprise. The lasso was magic, after all; it forced the person in its hold to tell the truth, so naturally, most people avoided it.

But the wristbands had a more general appeal.

It was the wristbands people noticed, and in an attempt at kindness or perhaps a desire to shut me up, they'd succumb to my request, straighten an index finger, point it into a gun, and shoot me.

I wore denim cut-offs and a white tube top, my hair shimmered from time in the sun and was newly feathered. I applied a coat of white paint over the brown of my clogs, added the golden wings of eagles, and finished them off with red and blue stars. They were my Wonder Woman clogs, and when I had them on I swirled round till I was all satin and power. A superhero. Strong and proud. Capable. Beautiful and protected.

"Shoot me. Shoot me. Shoot meeee!" I'd scream, till someone finally took pity, pointed a finger my way, and sprayed me with bullets.

62

We'd known Carol Johnson and her kids since I was a baby. She was the one who had been so generous, the one who'd given me the black purse that started my wondering about money. We were no longer living on the same street, but the Johnson family was only a few blocks away, and we made frequent visits to their house on Lamont Place.

Carol had five kids, the youngest from the city bus driver she had recently married. Her older kids didn't like him, and I lost my own impartial stance the time he and Carol took me fishing at Sodus Point. When I caught more fish than he had, he threw a tantrum on the stony edge of Lake Ontario, and Carol had to soothe him with touches to the back and shoulder. He was so upset about not having more sunfish flip-flopping around in his bucket than a ten-year-old that he refused to eat any of the cream-filled and glazed we'd picked up from Donuts Delite on the way out to the lake. What an idiot, I thought, as I plopped his uneaten donut into my mouth.

The house on Lamont Place actually belonged to Carol's father, who occasionally drove in from a nearby suburb to take care of things. The kids were close to my age and they had a yard. It was a recipe for success. We ran and played, sprayed each other with a garden hose, and made up our own version of golf, using baseball bats as clubs. Still, the Johnson kids had a love-hate relationship with me based on their mother's uncontrollable urge to give me things.

Carol was a giver in general, but for some reason she had chosen me as her favorite recipient. Maybe I let my need show more than the others, or else she still thought of me as the screaming infant from a decade before.

My mother had first met the dark-haired woman while walking down East Main Street. I was just a few months old, and in my mother's arms. From her porch, Carol called out, asked to see the baby. When she discovered that my mother didn't have an infant carrier, she removed her son from his, and pushed the carrier toward my mother. My mother put up a good fight, but in the end, it was my small body that settled into the cushioned carrier that day, while Carol's infant was relocated onto the porch slats.

It had been that way with Carol ever since.

She loved her own children, but taking from them to give to others was what brought her joy. She seemed happiest when she was giving us things — things her kids wanted for themselves, things her family could by no means afford to replace. Sometimes, I took advantage, saying, for instance, loud enough for Carol to hear, how much I liked her oldest daughter's denim gaucho pants. No sooner had my words reached Carol's ears than the item was stripped from her child and given to me, while the girls stomped up the stairs.

They spent most of their hate on their mother, but reserved a bit for me. I hung along the sidelines, guilt-ridden but clinging to the transferred object for as long as I could. Which was never long, because as soon as my mother found out, she'd make me return whatever item Carol had given that day.

"But Carol gave them to me," I'd say while crying, knowing the giving was wrong, but wanting the thing just the same. I cried until my nose ran and my lips swelled. Carol couldn't bear it. She wrung her hands, whispered for me to stop crying please, and promised to get my things back as soon as she could.

Kara was a social work student at a local Catholic college and had been assigned to Carol's youngest son as a case study or field practice of sorts. The boy sat in his playpen without making a sound all day. He didn't talk or cry or coo. Like all things her own, the son did not interest Carol nearly as much as those who were no part of her. He was nearly three and did not play. The social work student was concerned. So concerned, in fact, that she made herself into the backbone of the family, even arranging for the children's move to their grandfather's house. Their grandfather and Kara herself were appointed guardians; he would provide the resources, she'd provide the management.

The Johnson kids would have a new home, complete with new clothes and new furniture. I was jealous of their sparkly new lives, but knew somehow that a price had been paid and was cautious with Kara, especially when I saw her eyes closing in on my baby sister.

Carol lost her children quietly, and she and her bus-driving husband moved to another part of town. With the Johnson family disassembled and moved, the house at 10 Lamont Place became available. And when Carol's father offered to rent it to my mother with the option to buy, she jumped at the chance. And once again, we packed our boxes.

We walked our belongings from Grand Avenue to Lamont Place in open cardboard boxes. Our mother's car had never been repaired and there was no money for movers, so we pushed our washing machine through the city streets. People stopped and looked and wondered what the hell we were doing. It was the ghetto, but most people could find someone with a truck, or at the very least, a car and some rope. A boy ran up and snatched a sneaker from the box I carried and tossed it high in the air, laughing. Only a little older than me, the boy had no shirt on and his arms were the tight buds of muscle common to city kids. He taunted me with the sneaker, wanted me to chase him, but my hands were full and I was stuck. Other kids watched and wondered whether I'd be fool enough to try to reclaim my sneaker.

"Leave that white girl alone," someone finally called out. "Don't make her cry."

I looked away, my face red. By then, I knew how to let things go and decided to focus on what was left in my box — a couple of books and few pairs of pants. I wrapped my arms around my remaining belongings, crossed the street, and headed to our new home on the tiny dead end.

part two **dead end days**

63

By the time we pushed our belongings up Lamont Place, most families were headed in the opposite direction. Anyone with a car got in and pointed it east, toward the comfortable ranches and Cape Cods that had sprung up just beyond the city's reach.

But to us, Lamont Place was great, a giant step up.

We had our own backyard, big enough to play in. There was room for my mother to plant a vegetable garden, space out front for a line of pink roses, even a big old lilac spreading along the fence line like an overgrown child.

64

As one of her first actions upon our new home, Steph converted the basement into a bike shop. Half of the basement was dirt-floored, and even the half that was floored was dank and cobwebbed. Though space was always at a premium, none of us could find a use for the place. Except Stephanie. She saw possibilities everywhere. She scrubbed the floor, painted the cinder block walls, found an old cabinet to hold paints and a newly purchased soldering iron. To earn money for a few tools and a flat repair kit, Steph raked yards and cleaned out other people's attics. When her shop was ready, she and Scott Matizzi roamed the neighborhood looking for discarded bike parts — rusted-out frames, ripped up seats, bent handlebars — and carried them back to the shop, where they applied electrical tape and spray paint, finally rolling out shiny, new-looking bikes.

Steph also claimed a corner of the backyard and built a three-room fort with slats carried over from an old firehouse a block away. As builder, she claimed the largest room in the fort for herself, and gave me second choice. She hung curtains and for a while, the fort became a place for secret talk. When we allowed boys in, Jimmy Sulli shared her room, Scott Matizzi mine. Scott and I didn't quite know what we were expected to do, but tried hard anyway, pressing our clothed bodies together, opening our mouths to each other, wondering the whole time how such cold and clammy touching could ever be such a big deal.

Steph spent the little money that remained after buying bike supplies and snacks for the fort to take the black and white tomcat she'd adopted to the vet after his eye was damaged in a fight. She worried terribly over that bad eye. The vet outfitted the cat with a cardboard collar and for the rest of his life, he was called Funnelhead by everyone, even Steph, who loved him and loyally tended his watery eye.

She rescued strays regularly, hiding them in her dresser when they gave birth, caring for the kittens as best she could, petting them when they were sick, staying by their sides while they died.

65

The dead end of the street was a fenced-in park that sealed off the street like a cork. The weedy lot was used by kids for baseball and running, by men for drinking and fighting, and as access to Goodman Plaza—a square of rundown shops, including a large grocery, a Laundromat, and a furniture store that sold pressed-wood dinette sets to neighborhood women on layaway plans. The pavement in the plaza was smooth, providing a good place to ride bikes and a cut-through to the old Italian bakeries where we bought sweets and pizzas when money was available.

Though I preferred to bury myself under a pile of blankets and read Nancy Drew and Greek mythology all day, Steph was always there, standing over me, pulling me from Persephone on a regular basis. Once she had me in her hold, she'd convince me to ride bikes to Tyron Park or East High School, or to find old sticks and a puck and start up a game of street hockey. Groups of kids headed to the park for sweaty games of baseball and football. We'd spend cool nights playing porch games—Mother May I? and What Time Is It Mr. Fox?—and street games of Spud, Kick the Can, and Hide & Seek.

Girls spent hours twirling bits of rope stolen from mothers' clotheslines. We drew chalk lines and played endless varieties of hopscotch. An older neighbor would inevitably call the police when games went too late and the laughter failed to die and a blue and white patrol car would skim down the street and ask us to quiet down, which we always did, at least until the police car was out of sight.

We learned to look out for utility vans and police cars. The fact was, most people on the street didn't drive, so any real traffic came from those who turned onto Lamont Place on accident. We waited as slow coasting cars made their approach. Strangers looked out from windows as if they were seeing ghosts and wondering where the hell they were. We hated having to suspend our play, and stood near the curb, balls set to rest in the dips of our waists, faces wet with sweat, staring into the cars as they finally realized their mistake, screwed up their faces, and turned back around in someone's driveway.

There was nothing worse than a utility van coming down the street. They weren't coming to repair lines and wires but, rather, to cut someone's power off.

Very likely ours.

When my mother couldn't pay a bill, she'd simply toss it aside, unopened, like a paper boat set upon a stream. As her ability to pay lessened, heaps of unopened mail accumulated on bookshelves and tables. Instead of throwing them away, she'd add each bill to the piles until they grew through the house like a mountain chain.

Utility vans rolled slow and steady toward our house. We'd see them coming, peek out from windows, and pray they wouldn't stop at our house. When they did, and a uniformed man approached our door, we'd scatter like roaches.

"Shhhh," someone always said. "If we don't open the door, they can't cut off our power."

This bit of urban lore was true for only a few days. Eventually they'd access the wires from outside the house and we'd suffer the pity of neighbors who donated battery-powered camping lamps and snaked extension cords through their windows and into ours.

We learned to jump at knocks on the door, cringe when the telephone rang. When bill collectors called, I learned to say what they wanted to hear.

"I think she mailed that check out this week," or "I'll be sure and tell her to call."

I became an expert at pretending to write down return numbers. What's the point, I thought, since my mother won't be calling them back?

I was caught once. Lying. By a sharp-tongued bill collector whose voice reached through the pumpkin-colored phone mounted to the kitchen wall and grabbed hold of my ear.

"Are you sure you wrote that number down, young lady?"

When I said yeah, she asked me to read it back. I stuttered and stalled; my face went red. I considered hanging up, but lacked the courage. When she asked for my name, I dumbly gave it, and she began to use it. Often, and with authority.

"Let's be honest now, Sonja, we never wrote that number down, did we?"

My humiliation was thorough. Convinced she could see me through the phone, I felt real nausea as I admitted that I'd never written the number down. Even as I wandered off in search of a pen, I hated her for her tone, her use of the word "we," the thoroughness of her power over me.

The phone's ring was not a delight for me, as it was for other preteen girls. Instead a ringing phone was a police whistle, making me stand at attention, pointing at me like a finger.

I never knew who was calling. It could have been Rochester Gas & Electric, Rochester Telephone, or the man who sold appliances out of the back of his van — though he usually came in person to collect payment.

My mother bought a TV from him. Steph had done the math and told her it was a bad deal. She told her she'd be paying much more than it was worth, and was being cheated. My mother knew Steph was right, but was annoyed at her interference. She couldn't have a child telling her what to do. So she bought the damn TV, and added one more person wanting money we did not have, one more van to look out for, one more reason to hide from knocks on the door.

66

It all came down to the clothes.

Don't get me wrong, there was never a girl so courteous, so clever, so kind as Nancy Drew. And while other heroines could dodge bullets and fly, they each had their bad days, cases of raw nerves, bouts of self-doubt, and minor breakdowns. But Nancy, sweet Nancy, was always upbeat.

Nancy lacked a mother, but had no gaping wounds (or at least had grace enough to dress them). There were no prolonged periods of sorrow, no sugared-up memories of a soft face and lilac scent to pinch at the heart.

And while she did not want for resources, she hardly seemed spoiled; any attempt at payment for her services was refused. Nancy was gracious. "You're kind, but no," she'd say, and settle instead on a token of thanks; a well-weathered bracelet, a grandmother's ring.

It was all so simple. So honest. So nice.

But if you took away whispering statues, secret staircases, snake charmers, and the intrigue of words like "incognito" — it always came back to the clothes.

The texture and color. The variety and splendor. The flair and utter packability of Nancy's nonstop wardrobe got me every time. It was the changing of dresses before dinner, the wearing of pearls and lace, all the talk of full skirts, capped sleeves, and cinched waists. A million and one silks: charmeuse and chiffon, georgette and grosgrain, organza, crepe de chine, and taffeta. It was the swirl and rush of soft fabric brushing against the hard edges of my life as I took in page after page of gossamer and gauze.

And had I been offered her independence, her confidence, her bravery and wit, I would not have turned them down. How could I?

The blue convertible, the square-jawed father, the nurturing Hannah, always ready with lemon cake and iced tea.

I could not have said no.

But had I to choose just one thing — select between Nancy's sleuthing skill or her endless supply of evening wear — I'd have pursed my lips and acted out an internal weighing of thoughts. But in truth, I'd already be imagining myself draped in silk voile.

Because with just the right dress, I might ignore the scene outside my window. With glitter-tipped shoes, I might walk around like Nancy, cool and bright, well-appointed, and just right.

So given the choice between a father and fringe, I would have had to admit that Victorian gowns folded out from steamship trunks would win every time.

Hands down.

67

Our house was number ten, between the Spades and the Smiths. The Smiths were next door to us, at eight. Unlike other families on Lamont, the Smith family did not attend Corpus Christi, and drove instead to St. Bridget's on the other side of town. Only their youngest daughter attended the neighborhood church. She was called Happy, and the name was something like cruelty, considering that her family was the craziest on the street. They could have been hillbillies, for all the banged-up appliances piled into their front yard, all the babies running around without shoes. All of them were speech-disordered, to a greater or lesser degree, so that their talk was neither pretty nor a resource they relied upon much.

Fighting was what the Smiths did best.

Not that fighting was foreign to the street. People fought all the time. Mothers smacked kids upside the head for spending bread money on candy or soda. Women let loose on the men in their lives, accused them of drunkenness and cheating. Men raised their voices at women, told them to stay put, pulling them back into houses by their hair when they tried to leave.

Still, the fights between the Smiths and whatever target they chose were different somehow. More hateful and regular. They resulted in bloodied faces and ambulances. Their fighting was ugly. But compelling. It glued us to windows, hands clenched — hating what we saw, but unable to pull ourselves away.

The Spades were on the other side of our house. Unlike the Smiths, they spoke well and often. Their car was parked just below our bedroom window and Steph and I pushed our noses into the wire mesh of the screen and looked onto their driveway. We were riveted by Mr. Spade, in particular. We loved the way he stripped off his shirt to wash the family car, the way suds and water pushed the hairs on his legs into dark swirls against his skin. That his name was Dick only made things juicier.

His wife wore stylish clothes and their children had the best toys around, including two fully functional swing sets and an entire collection of Star Wars action figures. Still, things were deteriorating on the street, and they were a young couple with options, so they decided to leave. Other families followed suit. The O'Connells. The Aubreys. The Dinardos. Anyone with a car that started.

68

When we'd returned to Rochester, we found that Annmarie VanEpps and her nervous little mother lived at 20 Lamont, and we were reunited with them when we moved onto the street. The Sullis were at five, the Rosarios at four, the Matizzis at three. All of them attended Corpus Christi church and, as a result, knew each other not only as neighbors, but as parishioners and fellow Catholics.

The church became as much a backdrop in my life as the street. Though I was anchored in the realities of life and death and couldn't bring myself to fully believe in resurrection, or water turning into wine, I loved reading stories from the Bible, and listened to the priest interpret them as often as I could. The softness of the church and her community combined and contrasted with the starkness of Lamont Place and provided a steady heartbeat and rhythm to my life.

Together they were home.

69

She didn't come at first.

My mother.

She stayed home while I made my way to church. Once we moved onto Lamont Place, I rekindled my friendship with Annmarie, and it was by following her that I discovered the huge old building filled with light and warmth.

Annmarie loved the place and the people. She introduced me to them, and gave me a recap of her First Communion: the white dress, the veil, the cake.

"It's sorta like a wedding," she said, "only instead of getting married, you get to take communion after."

I thought back to Lisa's old lace communion dress, which had been left on the reservation, and remembered the photos taken of the oldest kids with rosaries and Bibles tucked under their hands. Lisa had been smiling in her communion picture. The veil she wore made her into a tiny bride.

It all sounded good to me. So I scheduled a meeting with the priest and arranged a First Communion of my own. I had already started to attend catechism, and planning a sacrament gave me more motivation to learn the Apostles' Creed.

"That sounds like a pretty good idea," the young priest said, and had me sit in his office while he found me a book to study from.

I made big plans. I'd borrow Annmarie's white dress, clip two grass-green barrettes into my hair, and talk my mother into buying a pair of white tights.

It was only after I'd done these things, had the dress in my closet and the prayers on my tongue, that Father Shea walked from the rectory to my house one spring afternoon.

I hadn't wanted him to come, didn't want him to see where I lived, the mismatched furniture and scratched-up floors. I said it wasn't necessary, but he insisted, said he'd feel better about my communion with my mother's blessing and so sat in our kitchen and ate the boxed donuts my mother put before him while I perched on an old stepping stool and leaned into their conversation.

Most girls receive First Communion on a Sunday in May, but I chose the Thursday Night Folk Mass. I preferred guitars and jeans to organ music and starched cotton. My white-stockinged knees knocked into each other as I stood and read from the Old Testament. I destroyed the names of Hebrew tribes and desert places and, after Mass, went downstairs, relieved and laughing, only to discover that the communion party my mother planned had been stolen. Someone had crept downstairs during Mass and taken all the cards and gifts — gifts that the givers later described in painstaking detail:

"Oh, it was a lovely set! A cream-colored scarf, I know you would have loved it," and, "The necklace was just perfect, with crystal beads that shone in the sun."

Only the cake my mother had ordered from the Sweetheart Bakery was spared. A gigantic translucent sugar Host hovered on white frosting, and yellow pudding ran through its marble center. As people came up and described the book or doll or rosary beads they'd gotten me, I stood still in my pretty white dress. I'd never had a party of my own, with guests and presents and a bakery cake. The loss was strange, but a party would have been even stranger, and I didn't feel nearly as bad as I knew I should.

At least I could receive the bread and wine, I told myself. At least there was that.

And it was in the basement, after my First Communion Mass, that

I looked around the table and noticed my family there. All of them. Will and Anthony talking with strangers. Lisa with a group of teen-age girls. Rachel and Mallory standing near my mother. Steph by my side. Though I had come on my own, they were there, standing around the cake like replacement gifts. All of them, shuffling in, taking their places, learning to speak their own prayers.

70

Body of Christ.

That's what Corpus Christi meant in Latin.

Younger kids called it Corpus Crispy, and it wasn't as nice a name as the neighboring parishes: St. Philip Neri, St. Ambrose, and Mount Carmel.

But it was my church.

And when I wasn't going back and forth between public schools, it was my school, too. Because I had returned to the church before my mother, I behaved as though I'd discovered the place or built it myself, stone by stone — but in truth, the church had always been a part of our family.

I was baptized there. Back in April 1968, two strangers dabbed my forehead with oil, stood beside the font, and said prayers over me. The woman was pretty and young. A nun, according to my mother, who'd abandoned the sisterhood soon after my baptism. She didn't remember much of the man, just that he was a kind-hearted parishioner who felt sorry for the rust-haired baby with no one to stand up for her. My mother couldn't remember either of their names, but they took me into their arms, anointed me with oil, and became my godparents just the same.

My mother's Catholicism ran hot and cold. In fairness to Rome, the religion she practiced should have had its own name. It glorified mystery, but resisted authority. She opposed birth control, for instance, but had a certain appreciation for sex outside of marriage, and sex in general. She'd stay away from the church for whole stretches of time, only to re-emerge wearing a scapular under her shirt, proud of the tiny badge that guaranteed straight passage to heaven in the event of an accident or sudden illness. Her behavior ranged from embarrassingly devout (she said rosaries to cure common ailments like warts and ring-worm) to shamefully liberal (she advised us not to marry the first man we fell in love with; certainly not the first we slept with.) She learned her Catholicism from her mother, and who knows where my grand-mother learned hers.

Missionaries maybe.

Her own mother had been wild, making up her own rules about everything, but adoring the Virgin all the while. Her father, on the other hand, was a practical man, a woodcutter and a Methodist, who was suspicious of Catholics and was said to have driven away the un-fortunate priest who came to the house to call on his wife. My mother had both sides of her lineage battling inside of her, the sloppily de-vout along with the untrusting and practical. Except for St. Mary's downtown, where she'd had her only wedding, Corpus Christi was the church she'd always attended. It was closest in proximity to the various places we'd lived in the city, the hub of the circle we'd traveled. My mother had had every one of us baptized there, which could not have been easy, considering that the babies kept coming — even after she'd separated from her husband — and each child offered up had an en-tirely different set of features.

71

So many kids attended Thursday Night Mass at Corpus Christi that they sent a van for us. Rusted lesions covered the side of the two-toned vehicle, whose windows had been replaced by clear plastic and duct tape. The van shuddered as it moved and sounded like it was at war with itself. But somehow it managed to hold itself together and rattle its way through the neighborhood, scooping us up for the weekly folk Mass.

The van stopped on Goodman Street first, for Francie and her grandma, then made its way down Webster Avenue, gathered up the Morales girls, before it turned onto Lamont Place, and parked in front of number four.

Kids came running from houses, shouting that the van was here. Flopping onto the van's torn vinyl seats, we were whisked away to Mass, where everyone (except Francie's grandma, who draped herself in a black lace veil, and convulsed like clockwork during the Our Father each week) wore jeans or corduroys and was so relaxed that they moved from wooden pews to the carpeted sanctuary, the bosom of the church. After we'd professed our faith and the bread became body, we'd leave the hard kneelers behind to gather in a circle around the candlelit altar and celebrate together.

72

Religious instruction was an intimate affair at Corpus. In earlier years, classes had met in cracked plaster rooms, grouped according to age, and students were given lessons on the Bible and morality by nuns or similarly inclined women. But when Father Shea was assigned to the declining inner-city church, he shook things up. He pulled children out of dusty classrooms and paired them with the new parishioners who flocked to the church from the suburbs upon his arrival. Birkenstocked vegetarians who said "God is love" replaced polyester-skirted nuns who said "God is watching." Studying other religions, preparing Passover dinner complete with Manischewitz products, and writing poetry from the heart, replaced rote memorization of the beatitudes.

I was paired with Julie Augsbury. She was young and fresh, and though I followed her around like the tail of a kite, I was not inclined to follow directions. I refused to write self-esteem poetry, for instance, and was not quieted by matzo crackers and kosher grape juice. I insisted on choosing my own topics, firing off questions about premarital sex while she did her best to steer our lesson back to the prodigal son and the nature of forgiveness.

"Do you understand why the father welcomed his son back?" Julie asked, looking me in the eye, hoping the mystery of her question would snare me.

"Because he was stupid," I answered.

"Is that what you think?" she asked, her face pink.

I laughed.

She labored.

"What would you feel like if you were the other brother?"

Her attempt was noble, but I strayed.

Again and again.

She'd redirect.

I'd sneer.

Until her patience finally gave out and she requested a reassignment. She got a sweet-faced seven-year-old eager for poems about matzo and I got Sylvia Kostin, the fingernail-inspecting elementary teacher whose name meant serious business to anyone who'd sat through her third-grade class at Corpus Christi School.

Anyone but Mrs. Kostin, I thought, suddenly finding myself entirely capable of prayer. I ran to find the golden-haired Julie, eager to spout my understanding of the prodigal son and the nature of forgiveness into her ear.

"If I was the other brother, I'd resent my brother, be angry with my father, but in the end, I'd forgive them both," I said, grabbing at her hand. "Forgiveness is so important."

Julie shrugged. It was out of her hands now, she said, a bit of satisfaction squatting in the corner of her eye.

Older than my mother and rumored to wear a wig, Mrs. Kostin scared me. No way, I said of my new tutor, but by then, my mother was back at church and in charge enough to demand that I continue instruction with Mrs. Kostin. Sylvia Kostin. The teacher I feared and didn't want to sit next to, but who, it turned out, was patient and calm and, as she set a story before me and asked me to consider the nature of love, brought out those same features in me. She sat me under the tulip tree in her backyard, serving lemonade while I read, and whether because of her reputation or expectations, I found that the words that came from my mouth in her presence, though perhaps strained, were thoughtful.

"Forgiveness is hard to believe in," I said.

"Good," she said, "keep going."

Melting my mouthiness without making me feel small, Sylvia was serious enough to encourage reflection and gracious enough to forgive ignorance. She had converted from Judaism years ago, but not before she'd had enough Manischewitz to take the intrigue out of it, and so, as we sat in her yard, Sylvia returned me to the scriptures, revealed the poetry of the beatitudes, asked me what I thought.

73

The church had its own smell.

Sweet and musky.

The incense used at funerals was strong, and lingered always in the background, while the high sweet perfume worn by legions of old ladies seemed captured in the very grain of the pews. Candles glowed, and smelled like rain as they melted. The balsam of sacramental oils mixed with the sad scent of prayers trapped and beating against the rafters.

The windows leaked light, bled color onto whitewashed walls, thickened the air with their hues. I faced the great panel of stained glass behind the high altar, and when the sun hit just right, the window spilled its sapphire and scarlet into the church and everything was on fire. I stared at the window during Mass, imagining that if stained glass had a taste, it would be overripe plum, sweet and strong in my mouth.

The building's exterior was tangled with ivy, its interior split into alcoves and domes ornamented with statues, thick pillars, and stations of the cross. The church was huge, high-ceilinged and heavy. An ark, really. Thick beams supported the plaster ceiling like the sturdy spine of a whale. I was Jonah, safe in the belly of a whale, I thought, as I leaned back and looked up at bats I pretended were doves flitting back and forth in the rafters.

I was comfortable there. Except for the joining of hands during the recitation of the Our Father, which made my hands so sticky that they adhered to whatever surface they touched. I tried my best to last out the prayer, and sometimes managed. But mostly, I fled. From the too-tight, too-loose holding of hands, the flaring of group prayer — the movement of everyday voices from apologetic mew to insistent boom.

Hiding in the last pew, I waited for the chanting to end, then emerged for the payoff. I'd blow my hands dry, run out for the Kiss of Peace where, like a starved hummingbird, I'd flit from person to person, taking just a bit of sweet before moving on.

74

The communion rail lasted only months after Father Shea's arrival. He was all for removing barriers, wanted the altar accessible to everyone. Though in truth, the communion rail had already begun to crumble before he came; whole sections were missing or broken, like the remains of an ancient Greek temple. Still, it was solid enough to lean against, its marble smooth and cool, and while it stood it was a favorite backdrop for teenage girls who gathered before Mass, leaning their summer flesh against it, comparing fingernail polish, sharing lip gloss, taking joy in being watched.

The broken marble rail was also the place where the gold-guitared folk group played during Mass, strummed songs we could bear until later, in the basement, we'd gather, child and teenager — even adult — and slip quarters into the old jukebox, then dance to Rick James and the Sugar Hill Gang.

The Corpus Christi community was strong. It organized picnics, held car washes, sponsored retreats. At Silver Lake, or the Jello Mansion in Leroy, the old house with a pond and canoes left to the diocese by the inventor of America's favorite jiggly treat. We paddled in canoes, talked about our lives, made collages to represent our dreams, then confessed our sins to Father Shea.

Corpus managed to put a more positive spin on sin, and confessions were not performed in locked boxes, but in the open air — in the soft cover of a retreat house or in the flickering light of a candled altar. All but one of the church's confessionals were reclaimed as storage and loaded up with stereo equipment. The one that remained was used by the few parishioners who still preferred the screen, and required that their Saturday sessions for forgiveness remain dark and enclosed.

75

Margot Whitemore was a sacristan, one of the ladies who set up for Mass, extinguished candles, folded vestments, and discarded leftover communion wine. Unlike the Sunday sacristan, Margot had spark and poured Thursday's leftovers not into the designated sacred plumbing, but down her own throat.

She had attended college, never married, and was called "Mango" by those who loved her best. Margot was an odd specimen to me, this woman with no children or man to fuss over, with her own house, her own car, coming and going and generally doing whatever she pleased.

Margot and my mother soon became fast friends.

A talker by nature, my mother would engage anyone, anywhere. In Margot, she found a quick mind and an all too rare willingness to discuss topics other than men and children. They talked about birds and gardening and old coins. Margot had studied archaeology, and my mother, who had always been interested in things buried within the earth, could not get enough information. She craved Margot's knowledge on everything from arrowheads to bodies found in European bogs.

Margot and my mother began having breakfast at the Tip Top Restaurant after Sunday Mass, and going to see movies on a regular basis. Long after their return to the street, they'd sit talking in Margot's car. Steph and I huddled together and watched them from the upstairs window, wondering what they could have to talk about for so long.

"They've been out there for over an hour," we'd say with disdain, never stopping to consider that we'd been watching for the same amount of time.

"Maybe they're lesbians," we'd say, then exhale delicious peals of laughter. We served as our own best evidence that our mother liked men, but despite our laughter, a certain amount of fear lingered. We didn't need one other thing to remind us that we were nothing like other families.

Margot was generous, but too no-nonsense to make a fuss of her kindness. She'd leave anonymous donations of grape pies and sugar cookies on our front porch. Presents for each child's birthday. And sometimes, just before our electricity or phone was going to be cut off for nonpayment, we'd find that the bill had been paid or that a bit of money had been left in our mailbox, and we knew Margot had thought of us.

I was glad for my mother and her friendship with Margot. Their outings, the church, and its community seemed to lighten her a bit. At least temporarily. Certainly things were brighter on the days she attended Mass. Still, there were times when I wished she'd never come back to church at all. Like the time she hauled us in for family counseling with Father Shea, and we sat, lumps of various size and shape in his office, while my mother listed off complaints in an inappropriately chirpy voice.

We didn't listen, she said.

We mouthed back.

We could help more around the house.

As she talked on about how we could be better children, I found myself hating her. For the sound and force of her voice. For whining to an outsider. For taking over my space. I hated Father Shea, too, for his disloyalty (after all, I'd met him first!). When he seemed to take my mother's side by suggesting regular family meetings, and started asking each of us what made us angry, the betrayal became too much to bear.

I refused to participate. My mouth hung open, I pushed my eyes to the ceiling and glared so hard, I imagined burnt spots remaining on the ceiling tiles long after our departure.

76

In general, I'd become mouthy.

By the time I entered sixth grade and began to understand the way things were, I'd traded in my smart-girl label for smart-ass. I watched the funniest kids at school — those I most admired — and took notes. I learned the art of cracking up a room of eleven-year-olds with a well-placed comment or an easy joke. Still, that was at school, where everyone was a kid or a teacher, and no one really knew me.

Church was different. Everyone was kind, and I wore their warmth like a fur-lined coat. I needed them, loved them even, but I'd become bad anyway. Despite the fact that it was a sanctuary, or perhaps because of it, I learned the limits, then pushed at them.

Like the time I gave Father Shea a wedgie at Charlotte Beach. He was swimming in denim cut-offs while a group of kids played Marco Polo. It was a parish picnic, the mood was high, water was freedom, and in truth, men's underwear was becoming an appealing mystery to me. The temptation of the blue and yellow-lined elastic waistband peeking out from the priest's shorts proved too much for me. I grabbed hold, looked to the sky, and pulled as high and hard as I could. I knew it was wrong even as I lifted his underwear, but his shock and subsequent forgiveness satisfied something in me, so I continued.

While serving Mass, I sat beside Father Shea and moved my feet in fidgety boredom. I swung my legs in wide circles, laughed at the wrong times, used the altar as my own personal stage. I stretched my face into various expressions of pain or hilarity, tried to get people to notice me. All of which led to my removal as altar girl.

"I'm sorry," the normally patient priest said, "this just isn't working."

I was crushed, had not realized until it was taken away how much

I liked sitting by his side and taking charge of ringing the bells during Mass. I apologized and begged. How could I go on, I thought, without wearing a white robe, and washing Father Shea's hands at Mass?

After a few weeks probation, he took me back.

But I was also fired from the Passion Play — the very same Easter production that saw my longhaired brother strapped to the cross in the role of Jesus several years in a row. Anthony had never excelled at speech, could barely manage English, and the few lines of Hebrew he was given were a cruel taffy in his mouth, but with his long curls, ink-blue eyes set under dark brows, and ruddy skin haloed by a crown of thorns, he looked the part.

I watched him practice from the pew I'd been banished to, and longed to be Veronica, the woman who dried Jesus' face and was rewarded with his image on her veil. I wanted to be the pious and lovely Veronica, had memorized her one line, and could say it heartfelt into a mirror.

"My lord," I'd say, my eyes wet with love as I pushed a dishtowel toward my own reflection.

I'd practiced holding her veil time and time again, but always, I was selected as crowd-person number three, and always, I'd rebel with salt-soaked laughter until I was removed.

Or demoted.

At Christmas, I was asked to reconsider my position as singing angel in the Nativity play when I didn't seem to take it seriously. I did take it seriously; I just burned at not being dark-haired enough to play Mary, not being boy enough to play Magi. If anything, I took it too seriously, which made my relegation to the choir sting all the more.

"No," I said when threatened with losing even that small role, "I can do it."

This to Sister Margie, the no-nonsense nun who worked with ex-cons all day and was immune to charm. After one sarcastic saying too many, she took me to her office and wondered aloud if the part of singing angel was too much for me.

"No, Sister, I'll be good," I said, "I promise."

She was smart and tough, but underneath it all, a nun, and there-fore, given to blind faith. Had she been as shrewd as she was kind, Sister Margie would have fired me permanently, for as it turned out, the weight of my tin-foil and cardboard wings proved too heavy.

On Christmas Eve, as we huddled under the organ loft, wait-ing for our cue to parade into the church, I eyed the gauzy wings strapped to the backs of the other angels, noticed how fine their halos were — strands of silk roses — while mine was just a bit of used garland tied round my head. They wore white ballet slippers and lace tights, while I wore sneakers and jeans under a borrowed robe. They looked like miniature brides; I looked like a cartoon.

The comparison curled my lip. Envy and shame combined with an overall holiday giddiness that only intensified as we processed through the crowd of hundreds and onto the steps along the length of the high altar.

Glo-or-or-or-ri-aa, came our sweet song as we faced the Christmas crowd.

The swirl of giggles started out in my belly, and soon took the place of the Gloria in my mouth. Starting out small, the laughter grew as the line of angels settled into formation, arranged by height against a backdrop of alabaster saints.

The holiday congregants smiled and waved and were clearly en-chanted by the glitter of wings, the lilt of young voices, and everything was lovely until Mary Lou Sulli, the angel next to me, heard my man-gled laughter and choked on her singing, too. Mary Lou nudged my shoulder, but when that did not stop me, she became infected by my poison and began to giggle and lose her place in the song. She laughed. An accidentally robust guffaw. Soon, the entire line of angels shook. Wings fluttered as laughter overtook Latin and we crumpled to the floor, one at a time, a series of haloed dominoes falling to earth.

77

One minute I was at my desk, looking out the window, and the next, someone was at the classroom door, calling out my name. His face was a blur, as if his features had been crafted of putty, and I realized as I approached that I did not know him.

"There was an incident at home," the man said. "No one was hurt," he added, as the words were settling into my head, "but you need to leave school early today."

An incident, I thought, and while I knew the word, I could not grasp just then what it meant.

A couple of older kids were waiting in the office to escort me home. Neighbors. High-school kids who were done with school for the day. They looked at me from the sides of their eyes as we walked, but wouldn't say what happened, even when I asked.

"We're not supposed to tell," they said with puffed-out frowns, and I knew that they were feeling full of themselves, could see that the weight of their knowledge was like loose change jingling in their pockets. They looked at each other as they walked and I began to hate them for their secret. I decided to stop asking and instead simply picked up my pace, finally breaking into a trot.

"Don't worry," they called, their voices taking on the tones of high drama, "it's nothing too bad."

It wasn't until I'd rounded the corner from Webster Avenue to Lamont Place that I saw the fire engines lining the street.

A fire, I thought. There's been a fire.

An incident.

The street was filled with people who had gathered and stood huddled and staring at the dark smoke coming from the windows of our house. I was welcomed into the crowd with pats to the shoulder and hugs. "It's okay," everyone kept saying, "things will be just fine."

I watched as firemen went in and out of the house, then followed the smoke to its source, took in the bashed-in windows and black stains running down the gold shingles.

Steph walked over and told me what had happened.

Lisa had been working on crafts. She'd been on a craft kick for months, in fact, using matches to burn the edges of pictures of Holly Hobbie or speckled fawns, then shellacking them to hunks of wood and mounting them onto walls. She created plaques to hang in her room and anywhere else she could find space. That day, it seems, she'd laced up the edge of some cute thing, thrown her match into a waste-basket, then gone downstairs for a bath. While she bathed, the match rekindled itself and started a fire.

I looked around for my oldest sister. Lisa was nowhere in sight. Steph said she'd been crying.

"Why?" I asked. Nothing ever seemed to bother Lisa. She walked around the house with a stiff back and a dark look. I barely spoke to her for fear of incurring her wrath, and had not seen her cry since Albion so many years before, when the kids on the bus had teased us for being poor.

"She feels guilty," Steph said. "All our stuff is ruined, and she thinks it's her fault."

I looked at the house again as things began to be hauled out front. People shook their heads at our losses, and the atmosphere was heavy, until talk turned to the small Bible that had been handed out of the house.

"Everything was burnt to a crisp," the neighbors said, "metal furniture, clothes, everything — except a Bible."

Their eyes glowed as they began to celebrate the magic of the book's survival. Even my mother seemed hungry for a miracle. She took the "Good News" Bible into her hands, flipped through the onion-skin pages, a smile lighting her face.

78

The school psychologist leaned in, asked if I was angry.

I shrugged.

He asked if I liked school.

I nodded.

He asked if I liked reading.

I nodded.

He asked if I liked to play sports.

My head tipped, then returned to its socket.

"Which ones?" he wanted to know.

"Baseball and street hockey," I said. "Sometimes football."

"Tackle or touch?"

When I said both, he asked what position I liked in baseball, and when I said pitching, he asked why that might be, and after I said I liked throwing, he said "hmmmm" and asked whether I liked to throw the ball hard or soft.

"Hard," I said.

"Hmmmm," he said again, this time with more emphasis, then leaned back into the chair with the orange plastic cushion. The chair creaked as he pushed his pen between his lips and looked at me as though I were a bug that had just crept into his kitchen. I sat still, wondering why he'd plucked me from class.

Earlier that year, a similarly inclined man had pulled me from class to inquire about the blisters on my arm — blisters I hadn't even noticed until he and the nurse had pointed and looked hard at my face for an answer. "I don't know," I answered, mush-mouthed, only to realize halfway through the interview that the blisters must have come from sleeping near the radiator; my arm often flopped onto it while I slept, and sometimes burned. I told them that we had radiators, that we pushed our mattresses against them in winter. They seemed only partly satisfied by the radiator-burn explanation, but let me go. So, sitting in front of the man in the creaky orange chair, I wondered whether perhaps I had another blister on my arm.

One I hadn't noticed.

The blisters really had come from the radiator, but clearly there was the look of a liar about my face, a certain dip and tug in the eyes often mistaken for guilt.

"So you like to throw things, do you?"

I looked around the tidy office for clues to the right answer, and, seeing none, decided to take his lead.

I nodded.

"Is that why you kept slamming the door at Ms. McDonough's last night — even after she expressly told you not to?"

At the mention of "Ms. McDonough," my mind caught up, and finally, I understood.

I was living with Kara McDonough and the Johnson children. Ever since the fire, the family had been split up during renovations, and Steph and I had been assigned to Kara's place.

He repeated his question, "Is that why you disobeyed Ms. McDonough?"

"I guess so."

I slept in Vicky Johnson's room, where the night before, she and I had talked about boys and clothes and kissing — what made some French and some just plain kissing.

I had closed the door, though Kara had said not to. Her ears must have caught the click of the door as soon as it shut, because two seconds later, the door was reopened, with Kara standing there, staring at us as if an apology was expected.

"God, can't we have some privacy?" I said and sucked my teeth.

Kara said she wanted the door open, and when I asked why, she answered that's just how things were, and I'd better get used to following rules.

Kara was strong—a social worker who spent her days looking into swollen faces and sad stories. Unrelenting lines were painted onto her broad Irish face.

Me, I had nothing but my mouth to back me up.

My mouth, and the overwhelming desire to try Vicky's blusher in private, to ask about what boys say when they're trying to get up under her shirt, to listen to Blondie's "Heart of Glass" while prancing around in high heels and pink satin shorts.

So, once again, I closed the door.

And Kara, strong-willed and silent, opened it.

I closed.

She opened.

Back and forth. Over and over, until she grew tired and left the door closed, so that I thought I'd won, only to find the door off its hinges when we woke.

We had giggled that morning and Kara seemed only mildly annoyed, so I thought it was done, but clearly, I was wrong, because there I was, sitting in front of a blunt-faced man who seemed to know all about the door and Kara, and was asking whether I liked to throw a ball hard or soft.

Now that I knew why I was there, I explained.

I admitted to being angry that the fire had consumed my entire bedroom, including the new maple bunk-bed set my mother had just taken off layaway. I said I missed my family, my street, all my old things, and that's why I was behaving badly.

He nodded his head and believed.

Though I was lying. The fact was, I loved Kara's house — the well-stocked fridge, the sparkling microwave, piles of clean towels. New clothes had replaced worn plaid pants and a "Put the Lid on Rats" T-shirt featuring a flesh-tailed rodent creeping his way into an open garbage can. The toothy critter was a free decal given to city kids to enlist their support in Rochester's antirat campaign. I'd ironed the rat and his garbage can onto a white T-shirt and wore it till the rat was cracked and the cotton gray. Gone now, the rat shirt had been replaced by crisp whites and yellows, turtlenecks with rainbow decals.

In truth, my life had only improved at Kara's. After all, Steph was the only one I'd ever really needed, and she was right there with me. With all the bright walls and balanced meals, Kara's suburban neighborhood was like a TV commercial for laundry soap.

Still, the psychologist nodded and talked about separation from family and how hard it could be, and I hung my head and tried to look sad, but the only sadness I could conjure was the memory of Steph's pile in the front yard.

To stop the blaze, the firemen had hosed out our upstairs, and the pile of gifts that Steph had saved all summer to buy slid out from under her bed through a blown-out window and landed with a slap on the front lawn.

That she had a pile of gifts hidden under her bed, waiting to be given on Christmas day. That she'd raked yard after yard, shoveled driveway after driveway, to earn the money. That all those presents had become flat, wet piles melting into the earth, more ashes than gifts. That her face never crumpled over such things (even as I howled over the loss of a double-belt — the one I'd bought at Larry's Bootery after raking only two lawns). Only these things made me sad.

I thought of my strong sister, of her kindness, and her losses. And other than these things, I could think of nothing so bad about our house catching fire.

But I said I missed Lamont Place anyway. Because it explained the door, and the man in front of me with the flat-lined smile was waiting for an answer. I looked at the floor while he leaned forward in his creaky chair, forced what he must have imagined to be a concerned look into his eyes, touched my shoulder, and let me go.

79

Liam and Maria were my friends. My elegant European friends. Liam, with a dark beard and a voice that smiled, and Maria, his high-talking, fashionable wife. They were friends I'd made on my own. Worldly friends, whose company made me forget the piles of dirty dishes and stacks of unpaid bills back at home. Maria, who had been a teacher in England, volunteered at the Corpus Christi School, where I twisted my legs into pretzels during lunch breaks, spun round in my plaid jumper, and talked to her as intelligently as possible about music and clothes. Soon, she and Liam began to take me out after Mass, to Durand Eastman Park, to their apartment, or the string of funky shops in another section of the city. I soaked up their company, visited as often as I could, flying away from my neighborhood on the white ten-speed Lisa had abandoned when she left for the army. And somehow, as I peddled my way to them, I was convinced that they found me as charming and sophisticated as I found them.

80

Alone in the dark room, I tried to remember what she'd said. My mother. Her mouth ran like the wildest of rivers, untamed and splashing, soaking whatever it touched, so that I spent much of my time trying to keep dry. After tonight's Mass, I'd recognized her voice and followed it until I found her standing with Liam and Maria. My friends. She'd never even met them. Until that night. And now there she was, laughing, calling me over, but not before she'd leaned into them and whispered something, exposing them to the clumsy girl she saw in my approach. And I saw, as I walked closer, that their eyes had changed toward me. They saw me as she did. Awkward. A child. Their faces were moist with laughter, and I wondered what embarrassing thing my mother had told them.

I remembered only their faces, their laughter, my turning and running from the church basement, rounding the corner, pushing past a strawberry-haired parishioner in a prairie dress, ringleted child clinging to the bottom of her quilted skirt. Both seemed suspended — their milky skin and red hair splashing in the air as I passed.

I stepped into the vestry, ran through the musty corridor behind the altar, into the side sacristy, where I scrunched into a ball and fell into the large closet. I pushed one hand over my mouth to smother the rattle of my breath and another over my nose to block the smell of lemon oil, candle wax, and dust. When my breathing slowed and the fear of sneezing had passed, I looked at the open doors and decided them a liability. I leaned forward and tried closing them, but my arms were too short and I managed to pull only one door shut, while the other remained cracked enough to allow a soft shoot of light inside.

The cupboard ran floor to ceiling, and was so old its wood was closer to black than brown. It took up an entire wall of the room and contained vestments used for Mass. The white robes of altar servers fell from hangers and brushed against my face as I folded myself deep into the cupboard.

I didn't want to be found. Not yet.

I knew the place, but it hardly mattered. As an altar girl, I stood in this room and slipped white cotton robes over my head once or twice a weekend. The youth group met here sometimes, too, all of us crammed together to plan church dances and car washes. But it was different tonight. Cold and dark. Crowded. With more statues than usual.

It was the night before Easter, and the statues removed from the pedestals on Good Friday lined the walls of the room, awaiting their return to the altar. Through the crack of the cupboard door, I eyeballed Joseph, the carpenter. Though I'd never found him especially worthy of devotion, hovering on his pastel-hued globe, face as powdered and pretty as a girl's, he had never seemed unkind before either. But that night, he seemed put out, and downright nasty.

The light filtering into the room grew duller, speckled and brown. The church was emptying now, only a few people remaining in their pews, bent at the knee, praying hard for Jesus' return. Most people were down in the basement, clustered and milling, eating sweets and drinking thin coffee, swapping news, wishing each other a happy Easter.

She was down there, too. My mother. Perhaps still talking with Liam and Maria. She had not yet come to find me, had probably not yet realized my flight.

I don't know how much time passed before I heard her call my name. The sound of her wanting me came in from the window near the parking lot and it was sweet, but I punished her by plugging my ears with my fists and curling deeper into the cupboard. Eventually her voice faded and someone said, "Don't worry, Therese — she's probably gone home by now."

After a series of good-byes and car doors slamming, I listened to the sound of drivers pulling away, one at a time.

The brown light diminished as candles were extinguished out on the altar. I reached into the pocket of my pink corduroys and found the thin white taper and its tiny cardboard drip-tray taken from the vigil Mass. I had no way to light it, but was glad for its company as I moved from the cupboard toward the center of the room.

I sat in a chair. One lined in velvet. A throne, really. The one Pontius Pilate sat on in the annual Passion Play, the one my brother Anthony was brought before in those years when he'd played Jesus. My legs dangled from the chair and I noticed the doll-sized plaster Christ child lying at one of its ornate feet, swaddled by a blanket of pale blue paint. A crack ran alongside his pink-cheeked plaster face and I looked away, to the statue of the black saint, tiny bird held in his dark hands. St. Martin de Porres. I remembered his name from school, then moved my eyes from his peeling skin to the life-sized crucifix resting against the wall. Jesus was on it, suffering. This was the crucifix used on Good Friday, the same bloodied feet lines of old ladies bent to kiss. Dusty boxes filled with blue glass candles lined the wall and waited to be placed as offerings beneath Mary. I caressed the candle in my pocket and longed for the sight of the sweet-faced Virgin. But she was still in the church. Covered with cloth as she mourned for her child. Out in the church with no one for company but the bone-dry gospel writers.

The house on the dead end had been repaired, and we were all together again. I was in the sixth grade. I still enjoyed my favorite things, school and time with Stephanie. I read and she dragged me out for bike rides and street hockey. But ever since my return from Kara's house, I felt different. I had found a pimple on my face at Kara's and when I asked her what it was, she had laughed. "Someone's becoming a teenager," she'd said.

I wasn't sure what I was becoming; I only knew that since my return to Lamont Place, I had less patience for the empty refrigerator, and a tougher time laughing off my mother's moods. Things were changing, and there were times I felt myself completely boxed in. Times I wanted to let loose.

I'd run before. Something my mother said or did would settle inside me until every part of my body demanded flight. So I'd run. And run. Until I got tired, or hungry, or scared. I'd run in circles usually, careful not to stray too far. I wanted escape, but not so perfect an escape I'd be deprived of the worry on her face. I didn't want to miss the sound of her voice as she called my name.

The last time I ran, I convinced myself I'd be gone forever and so took a box of fund-raising chocolate with me as provisions. "I'll be gone for weeks," I thought, "I may need these thin mints for survival." Hopping the bent wire fence that separated our yard from the back lot, I leaned my body against the cinder-block wall of an old warehouse and considered my options. I thought about heading north, toward Lake Ontario, maybe even on into Canada. Until I remembered suddenly that dead cats were often found in this lot when the snow melted each spring. Soft and sinking, their gray bodies became part of the mud. Too afraid to trudge forward, I considered crying, but instead peeled the gold foil away from a caramel-filled chocolate and popped it into my mouth. Then another. The candy had been intended to help raise money for school. Chocolate sales were as important to the survival of Catholic schools as Bingo. But as I stood waiting for the sound of my mother's searching, I unwrapped bar after bar of the smooth milk chocolate and set it into my mouth. Only when the sky began to darken and the air started to chill did I hear her voice, and by then, I'd eaten through the entire box of candy.

As soon as I heard her call, I rehopped the fence, nothing remaining in my fund-raising box but balled-up foil. My mother could have rightly punished me for gorging on chocolate we couldn't afford to replace — or at least shamed me later with a regular retelling of the tale — but she did neither. She only shook her head, quietly handed over a wad of crumpled bills, and never made mention of them again.

A sound outside stopped my thoughts. She was there again, I realized. In the parking lot. She must have asked someone for a ride and come back to the church. It was completely dark in the room when I heard her calling my name. My heart leapt, and I was halfway to shouting when pride cemented me. I listened to her calling—all laughter evaporated from her voice as she wandered the edge of the parking lot, sifting through shrub and weed, saying my name over and over, separated by only a panel of stained glass.

I bit my lip until her voice trailed off and I heard the car pull away. Then, before I even had time to indulge my regret, I heard something, the scraping of metal. From inside the church. I fell to the floor near a log of rolled carpet and squeezed my eyes shut. The sound continued and just then, I remembered that bats were known to roost in that room. I conjured up images of wings stuck in my hair until I deciphered the sound—the jingle of keys. Someone was locking up the church. Locking this room. I hugged the roll of carpet, but, for some reason, did not cry out.

Instead I sobbed. I hated myself and the room with all its broken statues, their stiff and hungry waiting. Only the moon showed mercy, and with its help I found the opening of the rolled carpet, slipped into its mouth, and slept.

I woke to the sound of sweeping. It was dark still, but kinder, with daylight playing at its edges. I climbed out of the carpet and crept to the door where I spied Jane through the glass; the old sacristan was preparing the church for morning Mass. Easter morning, I remembered, and suddenly wanted nothing more than to be back home with my family. Jane, with her worn face and threadbare sweater, had finished sweeping and was wiping the chalices on the altar, removing the previous night's smudges. I considered knocking, but decided against it, certain that a woman who genuflected each time she passed the tabernacle (even—as I saw then—when no one was watching), and had dedicated her life to keeping the place sacred, would not have taken kindly to my invasion of it.

I waited.

The minutes were cut with sharp nervous energy, but I waited. Until the clinking of keys finally came near, then disappeared back into the church. When enough time had passed, I tried the door.

It opened.

I looked out into the church.

Mary was draped in blue and glowed in the early light — even the gospel writers lining the altar looked somehow softer now. So I stepped from the room and sprinted behind pews to the set of heavy wooden doors, where I stumbled into the morning.

I ran.

Only this time, I was headed home.

Past the castlelike armory on Main Street, where kids played dodgeball among the tanks because the school had no gym. Over the railroad bridge, onto Goodman Street, where houses and restaurants and storefronts were locked and sleeping. Through the unusually quiet streets of my neighborhood, slowing only as I neared our dead end. I walked into our yard and headed toward the back entrance, hoping to sneak in unnoticed, praying my mother was sleeping and had somehow forgotten the night before. Her actions were unpredictable lately; I never knew if I'd come home to an erupting volcano, or a cloud of safety. Rounding the last corner, I held my breath.

She was there.

On the steps of the back porch. Staring into the yard. Following her gaze, I noticed the green tips of tulips planted last fall just starting to push at the earth. Near her feet, a mound of rusted frill had begun to uncurl into what would become a bleeding heart; its arching stalks would soon hang heavy with crimson purses.

She turned and caught sight of me.

"There you are," she said, and turned away.

"Can I still have my Easter basket?" came my greedy response, the only words I could manage.

She nodded and I saw that she was glad I was home.

Like our neighborhood, my mother was unusually quiet. She just sat and looked out over the small yard. And in that silence, I saw her.

I noticed that she was wearing the same clothes she'd worn to the vigil Mass. I thought of the short-legged polyester pants and her graying hair, and how often they'd embarrassed me — including the night before, as I saw her there, standing with my friends. Looking at her gazing out over our yard, I knew suddenly that it was not only what she said or wore that I feared Liam and Maria might have seen, but who she was — who we were — and for the first time, I imagined a night other than my own.

I sat down next to her and though we did not touch, we were close. Neither of us spoke. Instead, we sat on the rackety old porch and watched as the sun painted itself pink across the sky.

81

They came to me from TV and books and neighborhood health clinics. Cher, Wonder Woman, a pantheon of Greek goddesses. Poor Persephone's mother, the loving Demeter, seemed especially well suited. All were strong, all were capable, and all just a thought away from caring for me. Though I had a mother of my own, whose life I circled round like a planet to the sun, I was always on the lookout for another.

I looked for mothers the way other kids collected postage stamps.

I reached for mothers the way I reached for communion at Mass, hand extended, eyes to heaven.

I craved mothers like I craved bread.

And every so often, I'd get lucky and find one. At school, on a field trip to the planetarium, the art gallery, through the window of a car passing through our neighborhood. I'd see her, push my hair behind my ear, straighten my back, look hard in her direction.

I'd been stockpiling mothers for years, and except for Mrs. Dowling — the second-grade teacher who painted her lips a dusty shade of pumpkin and preferred showing filmstrips to reading books aloud in class — except for her, who had no magic and would not do, I had transformed every schoolteacher I'd ever had into a mother at one time or another.

I stared into the black of chalkboards while they talked on about sounding out vowels and the Revolutionary War, imagining my room in their houses, the pink ruffled canopy bed, the chest of dolls, closets full of dresses. Once I began to attend Catholic schools, I discovered that even nuns had their appeal.

When Sister Claire read poems by Langston Hughes and Sonia Sanchez and complimented my ability to diagram sentences, I found that my mother fantasies were entirely flexible. Giving up the idea of a frilly bedroom, I imagined a less furnished, but equally satisfying life at the Motherhouse, surrounded by all those plain and purposeful women, their tight clean rooms, their well-worn books. I imagined my hair cut short, the feel of my feet in Birkenstock sandals, and began to wonder how old you had to be to join up.

Mother collecting.

It's how I passed the time.

But as I grew and changed, so did my need.

By the time I was done with grammar school, teachers and goddesses still had appeal — but I needed something more. Someone real. An ear to spill my secrets into. A voice that answered back.

I wanted someone who spoke in calm tones. Someone with a phone extension, a full purse, and car keys. Someone who'd gone to college, who had studied anything ending in "-ology." Someone with done-up hair and belted dresses, who shaped her brows and applied lipstick. Someone who walked tall, wore heels, went places.

Someone who might take me with her.

82

Annette Bellaqua talked with her hands. The curls on her head shook whenever she argued or swore, and so the dark ringlets were in perpetual motion. She wore wire-framed glasses and came from New York City with her husband, Sal, who was on staff at Corpus Christi Church.

Unlike the women I'd previously selected as mother material, there was no sweetness, no saintly indulgence about Annette. She was smart and though barely twenty, had already finished college.

She took me to her place, cooked for me, went on and on in her down-state voice about the superiority of her marinara. Annette talked passionately about the Greeks, and took me to the Village Green bookshop for paperbacks, Japanese postcards, half-moon cookies.

She taught Latin to kids nearly her own age at the local Catholic boys' school and though she had a large and solid heart, she was barbed wire on the surface. She snapped her gum and if any wise-ass comment was to be made, it came from her. She certainly didn't put up with sarcasm from me and, in truth, Annette was so busy spilling forth run-on sentences on the topics of religion, politics, and feminism, there was simply no room to get mouthy in her company.

Annette was sharp. And in pain, brought on by the frequent absence of the husband whose job had carried them to the artless vacuum of western New York — the very same husband whose attention was lavished all too obviously on any number of other women in the parish.

Annette was alone, with all that poetry and tomato sauce stewing in her head. So she made room. For me. And I followed.

In Annette's kitchen, I opened my eyes and ears, felt the limits of what I knew begin to stretch. I kept my eye on her hand as she chopped parsley into green frill, took notes on which utensil to use as she stirred sauce, noticed the way her eyes closed, as if in love, as she read poems in Italian.

She was brilliant. And hard. Like cut glass. Centuries-old verse, modern thought, and words I'd never heard fell from her mouth like tiny flames. I was entranced. And for as long as I could, I stood nearby, watching.

83

Five girls, five fathers.

And only one of us from the man my mother actually married. The rest were reactions to that man — the one in the wedding photos, the dark-haired man with black eyes, slim build and a navy uniform, who sat and stood and laid himself next to my mother long before I ever knew her. The man whose face could still be seen in those of my oldest sister and my brothers. Mr. Livingston. A man I did not know, but whose name I wore like a skin, a man I cursed each time people asked if I was English or Scottish, and whether I was related to so-and-so, or felt compelled to share their slight historical knowledge with corny offerings of "Dr. Livingston, I presume."

"No, I'm not related to your cousin in Poughkeepsie," I'd answer, and when they persisted, I'd continue, "It's *just* a name — from my mother's husband, not my father."

They'd smile politely while squinting their eyes and trying to make sense of what I'd just said.

I played it cool, but in truth, I was jealous of Mr. Livingston, and of my three oldest siblings, whose last name actually matched a father, offspring of the man who had exchanged vows with our mother over at St. Mary's.

My mother said he was cruel, that I really had nothing to envy. She'd chosen him back when she didn't know any better, back when she was new to the city, new to the state, new to men. So new, she had thought his neatly parted hair and military uniform guaranteed her something. Back before she understood that there are no guarantees.

Despite his neatly parted hair, he kept her inside, blamed her when other men noticed the bend of her waist, the blue of her eye. He hit her. Wanted her pain to equal his own, she said, and made it so until, when she could take it no more, she gathered up her three children and left.

"Don't trust the first man you love," was my mother's frequent love advice to her daughters, the nugget of wisdom she'd gleaned from her time with Mr. Livingston, the pearl she passed on to her girls.

84

My mother refused to reveal our fathers' names. It must have struck her as personal information, too personal for us; indeed, it smacked of treachery even to request such details. Their names were like eggs in a basket, my mother sitting upon them while arranging and rearranging her feathers. She'd tell us their names when we were older.

"When you're fourteen," she said.

For my mother, fourteen was a golden year, the appropriate age for eye shadow, pierced ears, and apparently, the naming of fathers.

No matter how I begged and cried, she'd fold her arms and look away. No makeup. No earrings. No father. Not until I was older.

I learned not to ask.

Only she was allowed to bring them up. She spoke of our fathers rarely, and when they were mentioned, it was only to share their various ethnicities and eccentricities. Our fathers were her stories. Hers alone. And she delighted in her handling of them.

Steph's father was an Italian so crazy with grief for his dead momma that he kept a slice of cake from the last event they'd attended together (a wedding or a funeral) when she was still alive. I grew up imagining a slice of frosted cake under his pillow, its buttercream stuck to the inside of Stephanie's father's ear as he slept.

Mal's father was a Stanley Kowalski of sorts — Polish, blond and tall — a fine specimen really. He was hardworking and kind, but had some sort of meningitis, which had ruined his brain — a brain, my mother said, that had never been at peak performance to begin with.

Rachel's daddy was from the reservation, and sadly, everyone except Rachel remembered him. To her, he was simply a dark man who wore feathers and banged on drums in a faraway land.

My father was a sweet-talking liar. A salesman and opportunist, who preyed on women and was married to more than one of them. A bigamist of French extraction, but with a good pair of hands and a soft heart underneath it all.

Those were the stories she gave us.

That much, we could know.

85

"Who's your father, anyway?"

Kids wanted to know. Not many kids in the neighborhood had fathers at home, but most had memories, at least — knew who their fathers were, what they had looked like, why it was they'd gone away.

My oldest brothers and sister took their father's lead and enlisted in the military, one at a time. With just the four remaining girls and my mother at home, we seemed complete. We rarely thought about fathers.

Until someone asked.

I became an expert at changing the subject. In school, I made up names for certain branches of the family tree exercise that came with painful regularity each year. I fashioned Father's Day cards from blue construction paper and thick glue, then tossed them into the trash on the way home from school.

Mostly, I tried to forget fathers altogether.

86

When she was feeling especially generous, my mother would bless me with a detail, a description, a fragment from her time with him. She told about a visit when I was a toddler. He'd stopped by for something. She didn't say exactly, but I could guess what my father had come for. What else, after all, did the two share?

She laughed as she told how she and her friend Mar tricked him out of his wallet. They'd locked him outdoors without his pants, and while his chinos were in their possession, the women had picked his pockets for money.

"Diaper money," she reported, her eyes wet with pride.

87

Sometimes, I'd indulge myself.

I'd close my eyes and imagine him coming for me. And when he came, my father was elegant. I ignored the lying salesman part of my mother's stories, and instead made him loving and rich. Filthy rich. And handsome as a TV actor, with spice in his voice and a sleek black car that would glide down our dead end and steal me away on nights I tossed and turned and could not sleep.

A fantasy.

He was the endless possibility that came with questions unanswered, space left unfurnished.

All of our fathers were fantasies. We'd use the one or two known facts as rough sketches, subtract what we didn't like, and color in the details that best suited us. We'd create the man we most wanted, the man we most needed.

Rachel needed an Indian chief. She'd push her cheeks into a fat scowl, force Asiatic eyes into a heavy ghetto stare, and serve out a helping of indignation when other kids asked if she was adopted or Chinese or something.

"Chi-neeese? I don't know what you're talking about. My father's an Indian. He's as big as a tree and plays drums in a band." If the kids who'd gathered were suitably impressed or at least listening, she'd continue.

"And he's a chief, the leader of the whole tribe. I'm an Indian and so is he, and I ain't adopted."

Then those kids would see that her eyes were not just brown slants, but bits of earth on fire; her hair not a plain black wrapper, but a flag of fine silk. Once she'd set them straight, Rachel's skin dropped its yellow tinge altogether. Once she'd had her say, my sister was gold.

But she was just acting. She didn't know her father. Rachel had been only a baby when we'd packed the Buick and made our way from the motel room back to the city. She had no recollection of our reservation days and wouldn't have known a Seneca from a Turk. It was just the line she used to explain.

We each had our lines. Sensible but soggy sentences used to respond to the inevitable questions about how and why none of us looked even remotely alike. The lines were often repeated and intended to hide our shame. Shame that our faces didn't neatly match. Shame that our very existence was evidence of our mother's numerous sexual transactions. Shame that, despite so many daddies, we'd somehow ended up with none.

88

Stephanie and I used the mystery of our fathers to torture each other.

I'd point out the garbage-picking homeless man we saw downtown as a possibility. Long hair curled about his face like a halo of frizz. His black eyebrows were caterpillars taking a slow crawl along the expanse of his lined forehead. He looked like pictures we'd seen of Einstein, except that our Einstein wandered up and down Main Street, picking through trash cans every chance he got.

"Oooh, he looks just like you," I'd say. "He has to be your father."

Steph fought back with accusations of her own. The most disgusting options were offered. The old man at church whose hooked nose became a dead fish against our skin as he kissed our cheeks each week at Mass. Or Banana-Face, the neighborhood crazy, known to chase people with a rusted butter knife, who was said to have murdered his wife and even in the heat of summer, wore a heavy fireman's coat. Artemis Gordon, the second-rate fathead from *Wild, Wild West* (Steph claimed the more capable and handsome star of the program, James West, as her own Hollywood father).

Fathers. They were just a game. But a question mark hung in the laughter, and uneasiness sat in the pit of our bellies.

Like greedy baby birds, we waited, beaks stretched, longing for some clue to our existence.

Everyone was a candidate. The time Father Shea blew air into my face while trying to dislodge a bit of dirt from my watery eye, he became a suspect.

"So pretty and blue," he'd said, "You know, your eyes are actually kind of like mine."

He should have known better. Should have understood that those few reckless words made him my father.

I shared my conviction with Steph that night.

After sopping up the evidence, letting it soak her system like the strawberry Faygo she liked to pretend was wine, she announced her verdict: "No way," she grumbled lazily as we lay in bed. "First off, he's a priest, and besides that, he's too young."

My sister's sleepy appraisal did nothing to dissuade me. He was young, sure, but not technically too young to have had a child over a decade prior. I pressed my face into my pillow and replayed the eye-blowing incident in my mind. The closeness of our faces, the tenderness with which he held my chin. Why would he have said that about our eyes being so alike? It was some sort of hint.

He wanted me to know.

And what about his hair? Flat brown made copper by the sun. Wasn't that shade remarkably similar to my own? And didn't he always treat me like I was something? Hadn't he reinstated me as altar girl after my firing? How about the convenient fact that I already called him "Father"?

I shook Steph awake to share this more convincing line of thinking with her. She pulled tangles of dark hair from a face that remained sensible even in sleep. She considered my words.

"Yes," she finally whispered, "but you really think Ma and Father Shea could have done it?"

The question was bold. We squealed with delight at the badness of her suggestion. The giggles came in uncontrollable waves, and we smothered our laughter with pillows, so that our guts wrenched until sleep finally reclaimed my sister. I stayed awake and tackled the largely unimaginable task of picturing the handsome priest twisted around my solid paddle-bearing mother in a room draped with beaded curtains and red satin pillows.

I conjured him clearly: ruddy skin, body lean, teeth gleaming as white and clean as the Roman collar wrapped around his neck. My mother's face was full, her body spread before him.

"I love you, Therese," he whispered.

She stared into his face, her lips parted as if to receive his kiss, but instead of touching him, she turned, looked at me, and hurled an awkward grin my way. I shrunk with shame at having been caught spying. I tried to squeeze the image from my mind, but like the Cheshire Cat's, my mother's smile was disconnected and loomed large.

Steph was right.

They could not have done it.

The parish priest was not my father.

89

I was not yet thirteen when I gave my ears to Anna Torres's sewing needle. My mother had decreed fourteen the proper age for the piercing of ears, but I was unable to manage my longing. I tried to sit up straight while Anna pressed chunks of ice against my lobes, then ran a threaded needle through my skin as her long black ponytail swished about my face, making me sneeze.

"Be still," Anna said as she pressed her large body into me, but it was too late, and my holes were crooked from my sneezing.

My mother had forbidden earrings countless times, but on that night, in my neighbor's kitchen, I was sick of her rules. So arbitrary, and binding. On that night, with Anna's needle running through my flesh, I felt practically grown. And so, feeling the rush and swirl of power, I walked home, with lopsided strings looped through my lobes, found my mother, and demanded more.

And like magic, my mother gave.

DesJardin.

George.

She told me my father's name as though it were a gift, and handed over the one remaining photograph of him.

The setting was 1960s decor, drab olives and dark mustards. Two men and two women stood together in the picture, and I saw immediately that he was mine. My father had a thick red smile and clutched at the woman to his right with corn-silk hair and paper-thin features unlike those of anyone in my family. The woman had the face of a rosebud — sweet, but tight, almost shiny in its eagerness to please. Her eyes were an infant's, the pupils overtaking the irises entirely. She looked frozen somehow, as though she might have guessed what was to come.

His wedding picture, my mother told me as she handed me the photo, and the tea cookie of a woman, his wife.

My father's deeply set eyes looked adolescent, his smile forced — so that he seemed more boy than man on his wedding day. The sight of his clumsy arm grabbing at the pink of his stiffened wife was enough to make me stop looking.

That, and the mathematically impossible inscription on the photo's back side.

George and Lorrie married November 6, 1964,

Separated March 18, 1964.

What an idiot, I thought. Didn't he know that March came before November of the same year? I imagined him penning out the words while parked in my mother's driveway, congratulating himself for his quickness and wit.

"Ha!" he must have thought. "This will prove to her that I'm available."

And maybe my father's salesman skills were not so great after all; perhaps my mother exaggerated just how convincing he could be, since he seemed to have had no clue about what she wanted. He did not understand his customer. Anyone with sense knew my mother hardly cared about availability. She collected babies, not men.

And though he was my father in only the most distant of ways, I felt shame for him, for his dumb wanting, his miscalculations.

The photograph, the name, and the often repeated facts that he was a liar, a bigamist, and a door-to-door salesman with all the plasticity and charm that men who sell Kirby uprights are capable of having were all I knew of my father.

And that I had his mouth. A certain look sometimes crossed my mother's face as she took in mine.

"Your smile reminded me of someone," she'd say when asked, something swollen in her voice.

And I'd know.

90

Though I made up stories about my father and left plenty of room to imagine new mothers in my head, in the end, I was always left with reality.

My mother.

The endless chatter, the up and down moods, the small freckled hands. And though I was given to imagining new ones, I never said anything against my real mother — not outside of the house anyway.

Inside the family, I had no such loyalties. Anything she said, did, or wore was up for attack. I railed against the "mountain woman" T-shirt she'd taken to wearing. I snorted and sighed as she spoke about the splendor of New Hampshire to anyone who would listen. I couldn't even look her way when she took up bowhunting and climbed into a van with a group of camouflaged men and headed south to hunt deer or pheasant.

I attacked my mother's projects — her desire to carve an eagle into the shellacked coffee table in honor of the long-gone bicentennial, her habit of ordering bulbs from a mail-order catalog in an attempt to beautify our yard, the murals she painted on our walls — the way the swan and lily pad scene that had started in the bathroom had grown larger in stages until it threatened to turn the whole of our house into one murky swamp.

I sucked on a cherry Popsicle and sat on the porch rail with my sisters watching as my mother worked the small bit of yard in front of our house. One side had been made into lawn with roses, but the patch directly in front of the porch was hard from years of use as a makeshift parking space.

Her face was pink and wet as she pushed into rock and stone. We swung our legs and slurped on frozen treats and asked her what she thought she was doing.

"Making a rock garden," she said, and went on about her plans to plant succulents and make something pretty of the dirt. The Popsicles colored our lips and we laughed and cawed and kept our legs swinging while she bent into the ground before us.

But if we allowed ourselves to be catty about rock gardening and bad clothes, we never complained about the lack of food, the way she slept for hours and days, not rising until she was inspired by something greater than our hunger, the way her rules veered wildly, changed almost daily. We didn't remind her about calling a family meeting with forced conversation and plans for improvements one day, only to emerge a tyrant the next, an angry old bear who growled and swiped without provocation.

When she wasn't working or in the yard, she took to her bedroom and became impossible to reach.

"What do you want?" she'd ask when someone was brave or desperate enough to knock on her door, or "I'm tired, just leave me alone."

We learned to stop trying. We'd entertain ourselves as she slept. When there was no food, we'd open and close cupboard doors until Stephanie unearthed a bag of potatoes and fried them into slices, or sifted flour and salt and combined it with old Royal pudding packets to make cream puffs, or sprinkled sugar with food coloring and fried it in a cast iron pan till it crystallized and crumbled into pink candy.

Inside the house, I talked and muttered and hated her as needed, but when Sister So-and-So from church or the secretary at school or a friend's mother from down the street used a tone that put my mother in a bad light, I'd snap my mouth shut and refuse to participate. I said everything was fine, and hated them for implying otherwise. My mother could have been wrong a million times a day, and I'd have hated them anyway.

I was hers in ways that those with loyalties of convenience

cannot fathom. I loved her beyond words and clothes and yes, beyond even pain. The strangest of things is the way the hungry always return to the very same hand. The hand they know. The one that cannot give.

91

"How come whenever I hear about you, it's to find out you've been punished?" he asked. Bill McCarthy, a man with ankles as thin as dollar bills and more scalp than hair. He stood in front of me, eyes spinning, asking why I was grounded that weekend.

I shrugged.

"Well, what did you do this time?" Bill went on.

I shrugged again.

He astounded me, Bill did. The way he popped black olives into his eye sockets and then chased kids around Ellison Park during after-Mass picnics. The way, spindly though his legs might have been, he never allowed himself the comfort of sitting in his pew, and so dipped and bent during the standing portions of Mass. The way he'd never married, never had children.

My mother explained that Bill had been in the seminary long ago, but had to leave to care for his mother, which he was still doing. I figured his mother must have been older than dirt, given Bill's age, which was sixty or seventy, but to a middle-school girl, might as well have been a hundred.

"I've never heard of a child so often detained," he said, then teased me about the things I might have done to get in trouble.

"Talking back, I bet."

"Nope."

"Then staying out too late, that must be it. You didn't go home when the streetlights came on and everyone knows that's when you're all due in."

"No."

"Well then, I betcha it's your room — it must be a rat's nest." Finally he relented with a "hmmph" and said, "You know — I should stop calling you by your name altogether; from now on, I'll just call you 'punishment girl,' I'll say 'hiya, punishment girl' and 'seeya, punishment girl.'"

He'd laugh. Sometimes slap his knee. Then return to his quiet life with his unimaginably old mother until the following Sunday, when he'd wink those marbles once again, and ask what punishable things I'd managed over the past few days.

92

Bill was right.

I was in trouble a lot.

Just about every weekend.

I'd be sent to my room for hours at a time, or the weekend — or for a string of weekends. Sometimes my mother would hit me with whatever hard thing was within reach, but mostly, she kept me inside when she thought I'd done something wrong.

Being on punishment meant I couldn't visit Annmarie VanEpps, who my mother said was a bad influence. She said spending time with Annmarie made me act like I was better than anyone else.

I didn't argue the point.

Annmarie did think she was better than most people, and I suppose some of that could have rubbed off. Plus, there was something about the way her mother made dinner with items from all four of the food groups that made me cocky.

A few days at Annmarie's and I'd come home with a belly full of milk, feeling like I owned the sky, only to open the fridge at our house, suck my teeth, and complain about there never being anything to eat, and bam, just like that, I'd be punished for acting high and mighty.

"Just who do you think you are? Why don't you go upstairs till you can stop acting like you're better than the rest of us."

Or I'd stride in wearing Annmarie's clothes, walking just a little higher in red and white side-striped terry-cloth shorts with matching halter, only to get in trouble for borrowing.

My mother believed that people should not want what they could not afford, and since we couldn't afford much, our wanting should have been easy to contain. But my wanting was large, and I was finding, as the days passed, that the things at home were no longer a match for it.

93

I was the one most often in trouble. There were four girls left at home, but the others were less inclined toward outward expression. Still, I'm convinced that it wasn't my verbal tendencies alone that got me punished. There were other factors.

I was simply too good a target.

With my easily tapped outpourings of pain, I was a faucet for the thirsty. My soggy outbursts, the chains of "I hate yous," the howling. It was all so easy. In short, I offered the most bang for the punishment buck.

Or maybe it was dumb luck. Like the time my mother came home raging about something or other, and started yelling at the three of us seated in the living room. We sat tight, hoping it would pass.

It didn't.

She pointed and screamed.

Why hadn't we cleaned?

Why didn't we turn off the damned TV?

Couldn't we do anything worthwhile without her telling us to?

She yelled herself into a fit, and then lunged. We darted into the kitchen, went round and round the enamel-topped table while she followed on our heels, calling at us to stop. The more she couldn't catch us, the more she wanted to. The faster we ran, the harder she chased. We screamed. She lumbered. And even as I ran, I thought of Sambo's tigers turning to butter and wanted to laugh and share my thoughts with Stephanie so she could laugh too, but I couldn't, because Steph was turning to butter too, the tiger right at her heels.

"You kids — stop running," my mother shouted. "Stop your goddamned running!"

We screamed and cried, said we were afraid to stop, and ran even faster. It seemed like no end was in sight, and she must have felt the same way, because the next thing out of her mouth was that she only wanted one of us.

"The other two can go free," she said, "if just one of you stops."

"Which one?" I asked as my feet slapped the broken linoleum floor.

"I don't care," came her response. And the insanity of her answer stopped us.

We quit our running and faced off, us girls breathing hard in a line on one side of the table, her red-faced on the other. And what was it that kept me standing in the same position, cheeks wet from laugh-crying, heart-thumping even as the other two backed up, and slipped quietly into the other room? What was it that allowed my arm to be taken while the others scurried away? And afterward, once she'd hurt me somehow — once the crying was done, and my skin had returned from pink and was available to her again — what was it that led her in a tender moment to confide that she thought of me as special, more like her than the others, and then follow her confession with a bemoaning of the fact that she was too poor to send me off to boarding school a few states away? Why was it me, looking at a smattering of bleach stains on rust-colored carpet, who was most vulnerable, who found her declarations of love as stifling as hands wrapped round my neck?

94

The other kids got punished too.

It was rare, but it happened.

Mallory was hardheaded. She'd been caught stealing once or twice and was beaten for it. The whippings would have been shortened, of course, if Mal only had fessed up. But she was stubborn and refused to admit anything.

My mother spanked her as we huddled at the top of the stairs. The first few strokes came easy and hard, but after a few more, my mother's heart did not seem in it. Still, her head was as thick as Mal's, and she punctuated each smack against Mal's behind with the hopeful question, "Now, will you admit you took that money?" Mal kept saying no and my mother kept going, each slap against Mallory's behind sinking into our own skin as we listened, until we could take no more and shouted, "Just admit it Mal — just say you stole that money!"

But Mallory admitted nothing. And in the end, only my mother's tired arm curbed the whipping.

The baby, Rachel, might have had something taken away for not sharing, or for succumbing to an overall sour mood. But she was chubby-cheeked and sand-skinned, so much like the little girl on the fund-raising postcard for the Indians of Oklahoma that no one could stay mad at her for long.

Steph was rational, kind-hearted, and the biggest helper my mother had, but even she was occasionally punished for something minor. Fighting, say, or swearing.

My mother had her vices, but besides her occasional over-reliance upon the word "damn," my mother didn't swear. Except for the night Steph and I wouldn't fall asleep. After telling us ten times to be quiet, my mother was ready to burst. Had our bedroom been on the first floor with hers, she'd have hit us, but as it was, she was too tired to do anything but yell, which accomplished nothing, so she finally shouted at us to "shut the fuck up" which tore us up with laughter. We laughed so hard at the sound of our mother saying "fuck" that we had to shove our faces into our blankets to choke the gobs of air that came up from our guts.

Though my mother did not normally swear, both Steph and I cultivated a certain appreciation for the sound of bad words. We liked the way they felt on our tongues, loved the power of the forbidden, and sometimes made the mistake of saying "goddamn" or "Jesus Christ" while my mother was within earshot and she'd usher us into the bathroom and insert cracked bars of Dial soap into our mouths. Tears of humiliation and laughter ran together at the sight of orange bar soap in the other's mouth.

One time, Steph got the idea of squeezing lines of Orajel into our mouths. Orajel numbed babies' gums, so Steph figured it would block out the soap taste. We smiled to ourselves and waited for (perhaps even courted) the next incident of swearing, then squirted the stuff onto our tongues while my mother went on about no child of hers using that kind of language.

It turned out that Orajel cut the taste of nothing, but simply numbed the tongue some, so that watery suds trickled down our chins as our mouths flopped open.

Another time, Steph joined me in pushing the open mouth of an empty jelly jar into slices of white bread to make gooey communion wafers. We pressed crosses onto the circles of bread with a butter knife, then used the round slices to play Mass on the back porch. My mother stepped onto the porch at the moment I held an oversized wafer to Steph's mouth, saying, "Receive the body of Christ."

My mother said it was sacrilegious to act out communion. Then punished us. We laughed. Her rules seemed to come out of nowhere. What was laughable one day was a mortal sin the next. We tried to tease her into easing up, but she'd had a lousy day and wouldn't give in.

"Keep arguing with me, and I'll give you a few more days' punishment," was all she'd say as we trudged up the stairs, shaking our heads at having such a crazy mother.

95

Any attempt at beauty bothered my mother.

Beauty should be natural, she said, or not at all. Based on her belief, she wouldn't allow us to wear makeup or high-heeled shoes. She didn't do any of that, she said; she never did, and was prettier than each and every one of us, prettier than we could imagine. As a result, none of us learned how to apply blusher or curl our hair, and minus the cotton frocks and bonnets, we must have seemed almost Amish in our general appearance.

Aside from those times when I wanted to wear eye shadow and hoop earrings to act out the part of Sandy in the finale of *Grease*, my mother's beauty rules were not hard to follow. I liked clothes, enjoyed dressing up, but whether we'd inherited our mother's simplicity, or developed it out of necessity, none of us girls had an inclination toward excessive ornamentation. And other than minor pleading for lipstick or a curling iron, none of us really challenged her.

Until I met Michelle Labella.

Michelle was the new girl at church who came to Mass wearing a red satin sleeveless top and matching lips. She was a giant almost, standing taller than a grown woman. And as if that were not intriguing enough, she snapped her gum, smoked, and had breasts. I was younger by over a year, but Michelle Labella somehow allowed me into her company and began to dole out her beauty secrets.

"Wear red," she said, "always."

"Put lemon juice in your hair for blonde streaks."

"And if you don't want to wait for Mother Nature to help you out with those," she said while pointing at the tiny teepees sitting on the prairie of my chest, "eat raw potatoes."

I followed her advice; scrounged up a red T-shirt, drizzled lemon juice into my hair, cubed potatoes and crunched them day and night.

Pounds of potatoes later, no breasts emerged.

Still, Michelle seemed a beacon of feminine cunning, and it wasn't until she told me that Mitochondria was her name in Italian that I began to doubt her. I might have been a grade behind, but I knew perfectly well from helping with her homework that "mitochondria" was just one of the ninth-grade biology words she'd taken a fancy to.

"I don't care what any old book says," Michelle said while lying on her belly and filing her fingernails, "I'm Italian and should know my own name."

I knew she was wrong, but I hung on to everything Michelle said just the same. I mimicked her talking and gum-snapping, and one morning walked into eleven o'clock Mass wearing so much cherry-red lip gloss that the lower part of my face positively sagged.

I'd spent the night before at the Labellas letting them practice giving a perm on my hair. They used no solution, but twisted my hair into tight rollers. So when I walked past the statue of St. Joseph the next morning wearing tight jeans tucked into knee-high platform boots, my lips heavy as glass, and my hair sprayed into a helmet of frizz, my mother did not wait for me to sit down. She dug her fingers into my upper arm and pulled me into the basement, where she took a wad of scratchy brown paper towels to my face.

"Do you know how you look?" she asked in a way that did not invite response.

"Do you know what people say about girls who dress like that?"

Michelle and her two older sisters teased their hair, oiled their legs, and talked to grown men on the CB radio while their mother was at work as an overnight nurse. They lured men to them like underage sirens, then hopped into strangers' cars for slow and smoky rides round the corner. Even when she was home, they stole the keys to their mother's mint-green Pacer and took us out for joy rides while she slept. I'd sit in the backseat, hoping to appear casual as I clung to the door handle.

Everything was a toy to them.

Including me.

Michelle brushed my hair, said how much she loved the little wisps that grew round my hairline, said how much like a Puerto Rican I was with all those baby hairs sprouting around my crown. She decorated me while talking for hours about boys and the daytime soaps she watched. We listened to Le Chic and Donna Summer, bought matching shirts, and started our own dance group — the Sly Foxes. Michelle, her sisters, and their friends scooped up the foxiest names. Dr. Fox. Lady Fox. Mama Fox. I hated the name I was given, but knew my place, and so slipped into my "Baby Fox" T-shirt without a word.

Sometimes Michelle's oldest sister got bored and whipped up a crisis. She talked of suicide, pregnancy, or proclaimed her homosexuality — even started CBing girls. Sometimes she'd feed me pills — birth control once, and speed a few times — just to see how I'd handle it. After the speed, I felt obliged to fake a high for her, flapping my arms, jumping off beds, and rolling all over the floor. I was less motivated for the birth control pill and just clutched at the pink plastic case and acted sick to my stomach.

Besides being an all-around badass, Michelle was in pain. She was in love with Jimmy Sulli. She loved everything about him: the wide shoulders, the chocolate eyes, the corkscrew curls. They'd met at Mass and gone out for two glorious weeks. Since then, Jimmy was all Michelle thought of. Their someday reunion, their someday marriage, followed by their someday babies who'd inherit Jimmy's mop of hair and Michelle's green-flecked eyes. She even convinced me to sneak into the rectory office with her so we could type up a marriage certificate.

James and Michelle Sulli, I punched out on the keys of the old typewriter, giggling while she watched the door.

She pasted their wedding certificate to her bedroom wall, but it was not to be. Jimmy was in love with my sister Stephanie, who was everything Michelle was not. Jimmy couldn't get enough of how smart Steph was, how strong she was, how thick and black and long her hair was. To Michelle's great pain, Jimmy followed my sister everywhere, and Steph's overall indifference only deepened his affections.

Michelle's love for Jimmy soon turned to hate for Stephanie. She talked endlessly of ways to win Jimmy Sulli back. She plotted what to wear, what to say, what to try next. The more her plans did not work, the more desperate she became. Michelle was a soap opera addict, after all, with a natural flair for the dramatic, which led to sensationalized plans to rid the world of Stephanie. She'd trap her in an unheated winter cabin where Steph would succumb to the elements. Or starve. She'd put a chink in a chain, flatten a tire, or otherwise engineer a bicycling accident. She'd write a phony letter to Jimmy from Steph, saying she only had eyes for Scott Matizzi.

I stayed quiet while Michelle braided my hair and plotted to destroy my sister. It was only when her plans become more pointed that I began to worry. Not only would she poison Steph, she'd use the rat poison in her basement. She'd dissolve it in Stephanie's soda. She'd do it next week. After Mass.

We were at odds lately, Steph and I. Despite our years of closeness, my friendship with Michelle and Jimmy's fawning took their toll.

We began to fight.

Things only got worse when her period started. She told no one, not even my mother, and confided in me only after I swore secrecy. But I was giddy and weak with her news, and when her secret banged its way out of my mouth, she didn't forgive me.

We fought more.

The stakes got progressively higher: I called her names; she cut the internal wires on my clock radio. I told my mother I saw a purple hickey on the tender skin just below her collarbone; she used permanent marker to put a black dot on my favorite white shirt. It was during one of these escalating fights, with my mother between us, that I blurted out that Michelle Labella was going to sprinkle rat poison into Steph's drink the following week at church, at which time she would surely die.

My mother was horrified.

Steph was speechless.

And I was punished for three weeks straight for assisting with plans to murder my own sister.

96

So what is it this time?

"What unforgivable thing have you done, my child?"

Bill McCarthy was teasing, of course, when he stood before me, asking with his old-man charm why I was grounded. And I didn't always tell him. He wouldn't have understood the rat poison, for instance, or the fake communion, or the complexities of being a middle-school girl.

And he didn't care why I was punished. Not really.

He just wanted a smile from the one who was always in trouble with the mother who had more trouble than she could bear. So when he called me "Punishment Girl," it lightened the situation a bit, elevated my punishments (and my punisher) to the realm of normalcy, made them seem funny even.

Bill laughed.

Because he was kind. Because he had studied to be a priest and found bits of God in everything and everybody. Because he was an old man and I was a young girl and that was how he touched me.

I laughed, too.

I let my head fall back, forgot the pain of punishment, and laughed. Because of the way black olives bulged from beneath his brows. Because of his spindly legs and the way they bent and dipped, but kept standing just the same. Because his words gave air to my wounds, and healed them some. Because laughing was so much easier than talking.

97

The Diocese of Rochester wouldn't hear of kids being denied a Catholic education for lack of money, and so they helped families like mine, chipped in some of the tuition, asked mothers to work Bingo or sell chocolate bars to their neighbors, friends, and relations to raise money.

Nazareth Academy was a fine high school, and all my girlfriends from Corpus Christi chose it over Mercy (or at least pretended to choose, claiming that Mercy's recruiter, their brochure, and their teachers were dykey, though in reality, Mercy was the finer school, but sat on the edge of a wealthy suburb and cost more to attend, and very few girls from inner-city schools transferred there.)

Trading in plaid jumpers and a walk from my house for navy blue pants, a crisp white blouse, and a bus ride across town, I started high school.

At Nazareth, poor kids helped out.

We were given buckets and rags and shown to desktops and chalkboards directly after school. It was just a bit of work, and no one seemed to mind.

Except me.

The work itself was nothing, but I was an odd mixture of pride and shame those days. Though I still used my mouth to gain attention from time to time, there were whole stretches of time when I wanted nothing more than to disappear. I was overly emotional. Too sensitive, according to my mother.

"You get so worked up over the tiniest things," she said. "You've always been that way."

I hated being called sensitive. She may as well have called me crazy or stupid. But because I didn't want to add fuel to the fire, I didn't tell her how much I disliked cleaning after school. I didn't tell her that the reason I wasn't in chorus or soccer was because those groups met after school, while I cleaned. Instead, I said that I hated singing and soccer — that I'd rather do nothing at all than sing or kick around a ball.

Still, my mother began to make a point of my sensitivity over other things. When people so much as looked at me, I turned pink and lowered my eyes.

"I don't know how you'll get through life letting every little thing get to you," she said and she was probably right, because as I dipped my rag into the bucket of chalked-up water and ran it up and down the blackboard in the Latin classroom, my face turned from white to red. My shame flowered like a large bruise, with its eggy yellows and blues — it spread itself out and lived like a shadow just under my skin.

The Latin teacher had black hair and wore fitted skirts. She leaned against the corner of her desk, twirling strands of slippery hair between her fingers, flirting lightly with the only male teacher at school.

Mr. Berke-Collinge taught theology. He was as thoroughly modern and as thoroughly open-minded as his hyphenated name implied. He flipped up his collar, infused discussions of premarital sex into religious instruction, and thought he was accomplishing something by getting ninth-grade girls to giggle about intercourse. He was handsome though, and a good match for her as the two bent into each other and talked topics other than the usual Latin and theology.

I lifted the soaked rag to the top of the board and let it come down over loops and lines of Latin, wiped away lessons from earlier that day.

I was not enrolled in Latin class, was told by a soft-faced Sister of St. Joseph that the class was popular that year and no seats remained. I'd have to take Spanish.

"How were the students selected?" my mother had asked, knowing how much I'd wanted Latin, knowing my placement scores were high. It was unlike her to speak up, so I knew it must have been important, and waited for an answer.

"She'll do just fine in Spanish," replied Sister So-and-So, avoiding the question altogether. She smiled and told my mother that Spanish was an important language, after all, and I could always try to get into Latin next year.

I looked over the column of words before I washed them away:

dies

terra

fides

mater

I wondered what the words meant and wondered who'd be studying them tonight. I liked Spanish, but had learned plenty already, just by sitting with my friends, listening to their mothers sing in the kitchen while stirring rice or grinding platanos. Latin, I'd imagined, would take me places. Transport me to the lands of Athena and Persephone, Isis and Eve, and all those stories I'd stuffed myself with for years.

"Latin is for blancas," my friends from Corpus Christi said, and they may have been right, except that I was white, and the only time I ever spent in Latin class was after school, with bucket and water.

Streaking sponge-width columns until the entire board glistened, I looked back at the Latin teacher, whose hair was so black it looked blue as she ran it through her fingers. She caught my eye and smiled wide, which caused the theology teacher to turn and throw a charitable smile my way.

I turned back to the board, wishing the teachers would end their after-school chatter and leave the room. I hated being seen. Especially with a rag in my hand. And in my shame, I cultivated that part of me that wondered whether Latin class was ever full for girls whose parents paid 100 percent tuition.

And what if it wasn't?

"Life's not fair," my mother said. It was a statement she'd repeated frequently of late. She said it after I complained about something, while she watched the TV news or stood on the back porch, looking out over nothing. Her hair was short now and graying, and she'd push it in chunks behind her ear.

"Nope, life is certainly not fair."

She'd punctuate her proclamation with a shake of the head and a pop of a laugh that showed pity for those foolish enough to believe otherwise.

I should have known better. Should have cared less. But instead I cared more, and as I wiped away lines of conjugated verbs, it seemed to me that Latin was only for the best kind of girls.

98

"Hey white girl."

The Girls were calling. The Rosario girls. Sari and Maritza, maybe even Wanda. They might all be there, sipping on molasses-colored bottles of malta, snapping their gum, sucking down mango juice on their front porch. The large pine in their front yard blocked their porch from view. The Rosario house was emerald green and the color of the giant tree was so similar that it seemed like a needled extension of their home.

"Mira blanca," they said again, and I smiled and headed over to their place, a soft-shingled two-story a few houses from my own. They might have said "white girl" or "blanca," "tiza" or just plain "chalk"; it didn't matter, because they were talking to me.

I was the white girl.

My status had been confirmed long before I met them. I had been a paleface on the reservation, and then a honkie, a cracker, even a saltine, in city schools and city streets where my face stood out like a puff of lint on a gown of midnight silk. Even in Catholic school, as I dipped my head into our recess huddle, pretending to know more than I did about boys and marijuana, I'd chew on peanut butter and jelly sandwiches while my friends ate jarred octopus and talked of their *quinceañeras* — the coming-out parties they'd have in a few years — the line of girls who'd stand up with them, the dresses they'd wear. I'd blink my eyes and take in their lives as though they were publicly funded educational programming. I knew that being white was not such a good thing, and that their approval of me was an exception. When the seventh-grade social studies teacher showed *Roots* for three days straight, I became only whiter, my skin glowing like the moon as I took in slave ships and tried to avoid the dark eyes of just about every other student.

More than anything else about myself, I knew that I was white. Plain old white. Not even Italian or Polish or Greek — there were no vowels rounding out my last name, no swollen consonants, no grandma's language on the tip of my tongue. Neither dark enough to qualify as interesting, nor blonde enough to beguile, my long hair did not curl, and except for a thick pair of lips that earned me the unsought evaluation from other kids "you don't look like a regular white girl" — except for these things, nothing about me stood out.

"Hey blanca," came their voices.

And though I had wished myself anything but pale, had torn into my mother with questions about our ancestry, mining hard for the slightest bit of spice, in the end, I knew who I was.

"Hurry up, white girl," they called.

And whether there were two of them or five, they were the Girls. Hardly anyone called them by their names. The fact that they looked so much alike might have accounted for the group name. Hair hung like rope down their backs, they had full mouths, thin bodies, and were narrow as grade-schoolers. Las Flacas, they were called in the neighborhood, the Skinnies.

I was with them every day. Once I'd convinced my mother to let me transfer from Nazareth Academy and start attending East High like other kids on the street, I'd stop by their house on the way to school and home. I'd climb the stairs to the Girls' room, where we'd listen to music and flip through fashion magazines — castoffs from their older sisters, who had jobs and could afford *Vogue* and *Mademoiselle*.

The Girls were fashion hounds. It was all about style with them, and an otherwise suspect person whose hair happened to be en moda or who wore shoes like they did in magazines was all right with them.

"Ay que linda," they'd gather around and say in unison about certain pocketbooks, earrings, or hats. "Cute!" Certainly they were more in-spired by something on the cutting edge of style than by anything they ever heard at church or school.

The Girls didn't have much money either, but their mother was a gifted seamstress who fashioned clothes based on things they'd eyed on MTV. She'd lay newspaper on the floor and snip out patterns for Gautier knockoffs.

"Mas corta?" *Shorter?* she'd asked as they circled and made demands for the latest miniskirt or palazzo pants.

Even back before we were friends, when we still cautiously eyed each other, fashion was a part of our relationship.

When our family first moved to Lamont Place, I recognized the sour-faced Puerto Rican girl who did not return my smiles, but wore the same striped sweater as me to School no. 33. Long belted sweaters were in style then, and ours were nearly to the knee and belted around the waist. It seemed to me that having the same sweater and being from the same street should have bonded us, and the fact that it didn't could only be viewed as failure.

One time, my mother came home with a plastic container of spiced-up vegetables and a green garbage bag full of used clothes.

"Where'd you get this stuff?" we asked, as she bit into red peppers and corn.

"Oh, from Marta Rosario," she answered, as if we should know who Marta was, as if Marta were a member of the family or, at least, a fre-quent visitor.

"She thought we might be able to use these clothes."

They were still strangers then, but I'd seen the Girls and knew they were well dressed, and though dignity should have prevented it, I prac-tically jumped into the bag. Hardly anything was usable. It was all too small, even the platform sandals I'd have killed to clog around in were half the size of my own feet.

My mother visited the Girls' mother regularly, but that was her way; cup of coffee in hand, she'd wander into other women's kitchens, and talk her way through the better part of an hour, wearing down their ears on the virtues of the White Mountains, the taste of fresh berries, the feel of snow in May. No one was ever a stranger to my mother for long, not the Pakistani family that had just moved in, the quiet old ladies across the street, nor Marta, whose limited English was no barrier to my mother, and may only have served to entice her. While Harun and Bada taught her about cooking with curry and Pakistani history, Marta taught her how to recite the rosary in Spanish. My mother loved these connections, in the same way that she loved watching birds.

Always, my mother seemed most energized by things just out of reach.

99

It took years before I befriended the Girls.

It was in middle school, while walking down the street after school.

I'd peel off my uniform as soon as I got home and though there were no old *Vogues* lying around my house, I liked to make up my own styles. On that day, I must have felt a little adventurous, because I cut off some old khakis below the knee and cuffed them into pedal pushers, which I paired with an oversized men's blue dress shirt and flat white sneakers for my walk to the corner store. And as I passed their house, the outfit drew their attention, like string dangled in front of cats. Everything quieted on their porch as I walked by; their voices stopped chirping. The Girls were reduced to nothing but eyes.

Walking back down the street a few minutes later, a small brown bag crinkling in my grip, I felt their attention once again. I began to wonder whether my attempt had been too risqué. They must be appalled, I thought, but forced myself to keep walking. They shifted on the porch as I passed, their faces following my return home.

"That's a cute outfit," one of the older girls finally called out, once I was well past their house and nearly in my own yard.

"Mmm-hmmm," echoed another.

"Sure is," came another voice.

"Que chula—come over here, let's see what you're wearing."

I walked over as calmly as I could, and let them inspect me. They were pleased, and the next thing you know I was there day and night, watching *Sabado Gigante*, eating bacalao, learning to dance stiff-hipped merengues.

Their place was different. Except for the refrigerator-sized arcade game Steph had found in the *Swap Sheet* and traded for her Texas

Instruments computer, having it delivered to our dining room while my mother was at work — except for that game and the eight-by-ten glossy of Jesus with the pink-thorned heart taped to our wall, everything in our house was some shade of brown.

The Rosario house had color. There were plants everywhere, green leaves and slender stems twined round black and white photographs of dead relatives, circled the waists of mantilla-clad dolls. A six-foot rosary carved from tropical wood hung along the living room wall like garland, doors were covered with lacy favors from years of baptisms and weddings, a ceramic fruit bowl sat atop the dining room table, a suffering Jesus graced the walls, and old-time Spanish music scratched out from a kitchen that smelled of sofrito and onions.

Occasionally, I'd go home for dinner, but more often, I'd eat rice and beans with them. On holidays, I was there, in the dining room, table pushed aside for dancing. And all of us, young and old, let our bodies fall into fast, loose salsas, laughing and sipping down rum and cokes and piña coladas until no one could stand from the fun of it all.

100

No one told me the thing I most needed to know.

No one prepared me for it.

Not the way they prepared me for every little bit of my body changing—the way they told in advance about all the tubes and canals of my inner chambers, warned me for years about parts I'd never see, talked on and on about my period coming, what it would look like, what it would feel like, what it would mean.

"You'll be a woman when it comes," teachers said with patient smiles, as though menstruation were a crowning of sorts. I thought of all the girls I knew and how their lives were just the same after a period, only messier. I thought of my mother and my older sisters. No tiaras there. No roses, no glowing halos.

Still, they sat us down to scratchy filmstrips and clumsy health class lectures about developing boys and girls coming to terms with the strangeness of bodies that had begun to leak and groan.

"Looks like Janie's got it," said the filmstrip mother to her husband as she emerged from the pink-canopied bedroom where her daughter sat glowing.

"I guess our little Janie is a woman now." The filmstrip father smiled, his voice swollen with pride, as though Janie had just swum the length of the Atlantic.

Everyone laughed and celebrated Janie's blossoming. The buttercup mother and robot father held hands. Their teeth gleamed as they welcomed Janie to the wonderful world of menstruation. But to a roomful of kids without handholding parents and canopy beds, their words came out high-pitched and squeaky, in sounds that hurt our ears.

And all those visits from community educators teaching us about STDs, pregnancy, and how to roll the latex onto the shaft just so. All those diagrams and diaphragms and maps of our bodies. None of it really mattered.

While my own period was a source of mild pride as I told Steph and bragged to my friends and tried to feel like I'd been transformed somehow, it was basically a disappointment. My insides cramped and blood came each month, but nothing was different. My mother still wrapped a kerchief around her head and barked orders, then hibernated for days. Bill collectors still called. People on Lamont Place still fought. A little blood, sure. But nothing like the exciting transformation Janie seemed to have experienced.

All that time and all that talk, and no one ever talked about the stuff that mattered.

The most important thing of all.

Steph and I went together.

We had to get physicals first. We tacked ourselves to the end of a long line at the free health clinic near Monroe High School, where the nurse would probe our backs and scribble our weights. While waiting for Steph to finish her appointment so we could take a bus downtown, I endured a group of boys putting their lips on my neck and trying to talk me into a dark corner. But finally, it was done, and I had it in hand.

A work permit.

It was everything. Practically magic.

Small enough to fit into my pocket; the little blue card changed my life more than a period ever could.

I had always been a worker — even in grammar school, I'd sold Olympic greeting cards with Annmarie VanEpps, raked yards, shoveled the walks and drives of strangers. I had despised scrubbing blackboards at Nazareth Academy, but it wasn't the task itself that had annoyed me. Only the idea of being seen as poor had bothered me.

But lots of kids had jobs.

With a job, I might feel like everyone else.

I discovered that there was always someone willing to ignore the fine print on the back of the card and hire a fourteen-year-old, somebody who'd allow kids to work well into the night.

Once I started working, I didn't stop.

I'd quit a job from time to time, but I'd always find another. I worked at a fast food restaurant, H&L Greens' five-and-dime store, Varden's photo studio, Seabreeze Amusement Park. Ringing up burgers and fries, stuffing envelopes with flyers, spinning sugar into cotton candy, selling low-grade underwear to old women on tight budgets — these were things I could do.

101

Sex was nothing new.

I'd heard talk of it, giggled, kept secrets, and gossiped about it since I was a kid.

Way back before middle school, on the way to day camp at Eastside Community Center, two women with swollen Afros and glossed-up lips had asked me and my sister to roll up our pant legs. We were wearing our day-camp shirts, but still they wanted us to roll up our pants, see if we could show a little leg.

"Okay girls, let's see what you got there," one of them said, her speech heavy with drink.

"Come on now, don't be shy, let's see if you know how to get it going." Her face looked bruised and she was perspiring in the August sun.

Scared and obedient, I bent down and attempted to roll up the leg of my jeans, glancing up at them to be sure I understood the request till Steph swatted at me and told me to ignore them. I pushed the rolls of my jeans back down, and turned to leave.

They seemed annoyed at our inattention and kept talking until one of them finally tired and started walking away. She turned back to her friend, who had remained planted, just staring at our fully clad legs.

"C'mon, them's just kids anyway; they too young."

Her voice was as syrupy as her friend's, but she was right. We were kids, just ten or so. But even as Steph and I walked on, I knew their asking us to expose a part of our bodies and the fatigue on their faces had to do with sex; the pain of it, the commodity of it.

102

I'd longed for it.

I'd eaten chunk after chunk of raw potato for days, then weeks, all based on Michelle Labella's recommendation, and still my chest was as shapeless as every other part of my body. I stared and turned in the mirror, looked here and there for signs of change. Looked hard for the woman I was supposed to become.

Nothing.

I should have known better, should have known that men gathered on street corners would inform me, should have known that they'd give an "mm, mmmm, mmm" and "sure looks fine" as I walked by. I should have understood that men tucked into storefronts would notice the titties springing from the plain of my chest before I'd even have a chance to ask my mother for money to buy a bra.

Once they noticed, everything changed.

When I passed them on the street, I lowered my head. I'd look at the ground and keep walking. Past the fish market on Parsells and Webster where men stood around, hungry for something to look at.

They approached in groups or sometimes alone, hand and voice united in a sweet sell. Their voices were hot and wet, and there was a small part of me that didn't mind being called baby all the time. But mostly, I hated it. Mostly, I learned to stay with the Girls on trips to the store or church or anywhere else.

When my mom wanted bread or a gallon of milk and I had to get it, I'd beg the Girls to walk with me. They wouldn't want to go, but might need me later that day, and so they usually came. Two were safer than one, and three were even better. We'd avoid their eyes, ignore their calls, talk to each other about clothes, shoes, what we'd seen on TV — anything but them.

103

Some days it seemed like everyone was falling.

Girls from Catholic school, girls from public school, girls from high school, girls from middle school. Girls from any school.

Even my old friend Annmarie let a man with a girlfriend sweet-talk her. She quit school as soon as she discovered she was pregnant, enrolled in the Young Mother's Program, and began talking of nothing but her new life. Even when she miscarried, she still wanted her new life, and pleaded with Father Shea to marry her.

"Marriage is an important decision," he said. "Not something rushed into."

Annmarie pleaded with the man who had known her since she was a child.

"I won't do it," he said. "I have no faith that this will be good for you."

She straightened her back, pushed fists onto her hips, but the priest would not change his mind.

After he said no, Annmarie married her man at the town hall in Irondequoit, wore stiff white lace at about the same time the rest of us were taking final exams. Annmarie had her reception at the Ponderosa where she worked, knowing it was tacky even as she did it. But she didn't have the money to match her dreams. Just a white dress and a boss that provided an employee discount and free drinks.

104

We went to dances in the church basement. Other than walking around the neighborhood in packs when the weather was right and looking at the never-changing world from front porches, church dances were the only way to meet boys from outside the neighborhood. Boys who seemed different.

I met Sergio at a Halloween dance. I was Cleopatra; he was a zombie. His hair was high, his back was straight, and he smelled like falling leaves and overripe cologne. Even though he couldn't dance, I liked his small bright eyes and the way he pressed into me as he moved to Chaka Kahn, so I followed him to the park after the dance was over. When he wanted to kiss, I said no, but a touch on my arm turned my no into a yes. He pushed me against the fence and groaned his way into my long white gown. It was nearly November and I didn't even mind the warm fog of his breath, the pink of his fingers.

I'd been an Egyptian princess all night, snake coiled on my arm, eyes lined in black, but there I was, pressed against the fence, Sergio's breath on my neck, with nowhere to go but down. But I was strong. I closed my eyes, pried my body from the fence, and ran all the way home.

Danny was a good boy. His family attended Corpus Christi and I met him at the next dance. He had big brown eyes and curly hair and I loved him instantly. He looked like Ray Parker Jr., I said to anyone who'd listen, and when he asked me to dance, I'd thought the night was perfect. I sucked in my cheeks, twirled my hair, tried to look mysterious in the church basement light.

And it worked.

He loved me, too.

He called all the time, gave me roses, told me my eyes were better than the stained glass at church, said my skin was like milk. He wanted me to meet his mother, his brothers, his aunt in from New York. He kept at me until I couldn't take it any longer. I refused to let him touch me, didn't return his calls, wouldn't take the rides he offered after school.

Danny didn't attend East High, but borrowed his brother's car and drove across town to sit on the corner and wait for me. But I'd had enough of being adored; it had begun to feel like sandpaper against my skin. So I stood at the bus stop and waited, even in the rain, never once looking his way.

105

I was at home skipping school when I heard the scrape of keys in the lock. I flew up the stairs just as two voices came in from the cold. It was Anthony, just home from the Marines. Not recognizing the other voice, I wondered who it was until Tony asked, "So how long you been hookin'?" and then, a moment later, "How much is this gonna cost me anyway?"

A prostitute!

I sat at the top of the stairs and listened.

My breathing slowed.

I wondered what would happen and how it would sound. But in the end, all Anthony did was talk. He used his time with the hooker as a sort of therapy and shared his concerns about what to do with his life, our family, how hard it was to be home from the Marines.

"I hate it here," he said. "My mother's always on my back. None of them really get me."

"What about your sisters?" The hooker seemed to be probing for a bright spot.

"They're all pains in the ass, except for maybe Steph."

I had to hold myself back.

All the times I had worried over Anthony before he'd left for the service came flooding to me — times he'd been chased by groups of boys or had walked miles in winter without gloves or had stood up on the altar as Jesus, me biting my lips as he stumbled through the Hebrew in the crucifixion scene. Now, at the top of the stairs, eavesdropping on his confession to a prostitute, I was torn between wanting to kill him and to continue concealing my presence.

In the end, I simply sat there, waiting.

And, as if my brother's disloyalty and preference for Stephanie weren't enough, I found myself deeply disappointed. I had learned nothing more about sex — certainly less than having a prostitute in one's living room seemed to have promised.

106

Men lied. I knew this.

The Girls and I sat around swapping stories about what had happened to so-and-so — our sisters, our friends, our mothers. And if the evidence around me weren't enough, I thought back to the stories I'd read, remembered how often the gods were cruel. I thought of Hades and the trouble he'd caused poor Persephone with his sugared-up pomegranate seeds. I thought of Nancy Drew and that boyfriend of hers. Ned Nickerson was polite and handsome, sure — but in the end, she was always left saving him. Even Wonder Woman could never trust Steve Trevor with who she really was.

We'd gather on porches and talk about strong women and weak women, swearing we'd never be like everyone else.

When someone got pregnant and dropped out of high school, she was no longer worth the time of day. When someone gave in and met a man in the back lot, we called her a whore behind her back. A girl who let a boy come between her and her friends was nothing but a bitch.

We were cold-blooded.

But our cruelty was a prayer, recited time and again. For protection. Salvation. And hope.

107

It wasn't easy to pass those voices by. Hard, sweet voices. Voices that wanted me more than anyone at home. But I did. I passed and ignored, passed and ignored. Until it seemed I was the very last to do so.

And as my junior year of school wound down, I looked for signs of what was in store for those who'd listened to the health teacher, the parish priest, the message on TV. What happened to those who played by the rules? What was the reward, I wondered, besides a bit of self-righteousness and a smattering of pride?

Isis, Nancy Drew, the goddess Athena. I had looked up to them, had wanted to rise above everything and join them somehow. But as I began to think more seriously, I saw what fiction the whole thing was. None of them were even real, I thought, while looking at life unfolding around me. No matter how hard I looked, I saw no magic. Just swollen bellies and laps filled with babies.

And though I'd shaken my head from side to side and tsked those girls and their lives for years, I began to notice something other than disgust. Something else was taking hold. Envy. It blossomed in me, surprised and scared me with how swiftly it moved in. And when I was honest, I had to admit that a part of me was jealous of those girls, their babies, their men — the way their lives were laid out like roads we all knew.

108

Ruben was older.

A man, really.

With green eyes and gold hair and a tongue thick with accent and beer. He drove an orange Pinto with the flag of Cuba stuck to the bumper. He kept the windows down in summer, let the toques and claves of old Havana fall into the night, sent streamers of sound into the street as he passed. There was no room for playing around in the Pinto, but he tried to get up under my shirt anyway, and I let him more than I should have. I'd been careful never to let anyone close before, but I let him under my shirt and anywhere else he wanted to go, because no one thinks straight during a fall.

And I was falling.

The first time I saw him, I was hanging on the corner of Lamont Place with the Girls, laughing at guys walking by, pressing their fingers to their lips, making kissing sounds, touching themselves on their bellies and lower, saying, "Hot damn — you look fine."

Then he passed by in his little orange car and smiled our way and looked so good — tan skin and full lips — that we shouted back. His windows were down, a cumbia was playing, and he waved.

We didn't call out to guys usually, but with Ruben, we hollered back.

Because we were silly and bored. Because it was a hot summer night. Because he seemed safe: he was driving, and white. A good-looking white man driving through the ghetto listening to Latin music in his stupid little car. He'd be gone by the time our voices ever reached him.

So we called out. We laughed and turned round and felt high on the night air. And it was all so fun, until he made a U-turn right in the middle of Webster Avenue and came back around, pulled over to the curb, and called me over with a curl of his index finger. The Girls were laughing still, but even their laughter had grown thin.

"You better go on, white girl," they said. "He wants you."

I just stood there, scared. Of their sending me forward. Of his waiting. Of his eyes on my shirt, the one with palm trees, the one that had grown tighter this summer, the one my mother said showed too much of what was just underneath.

"Mira chica," he called, "you speak only English, verdad?"

I nodded, and his voice showed he was not nearly as white as I'd thought. Not nearly so white as me.

"Come over to here," he said.

"Come on chicita, I not going to eat you!" His smile was wicked and luscious, and as I approached I thought of Red Riding Hood's wolf.

He talked quickly and seriously. He'd come back in a few days' time and pick me up. He'd take me to a club. We would talk. And dance.

"But I'm not old enough," I started to say, and he cupped my cheek with the inside of a warm strong hand.

"Okay," I murmured, and wondered what I was doing.

When Ruben returned, he picked me up from the same place. I walked away from my friends wearing a skirt that hugged my hips, flaring just beneath the knee. A mermaid skirt, it was called, and as I folded myself into the ocean of his car, I felt more like a fish than a girl.

He talked to someone and got me into the club where we watched other people dance. We sat with our drinks and Ruben pushed his finger up under my skirt and pressed tiny circles into my thigh while he talked to his brother in Spanish and I made an art of pretending. I pretended not to understand what they were saying, pretended not to notice how thin his brother was from drugs, pretended not to feel Ruben's hand creeping up my leg, higher and higher.

I tapped my foot against the floor, hoped I came off as comfortable, and watched as blonde women in tight jeans fell into well-built men who grabbed their asses and planted open-mouthed kisses to the pulsing music. I said no to a joint, but drank whatever was offered, tried not to jump as his finger moved up my leg, and let him lift my shirt when he dropped me at home, let him kiss my breasts.

"You're falling," said my friends, who had waited up for the details.

"She's falling," said the Girls to their mother, who said to be careful with los Cubanos.

I'm falling, I said to myself as I retraced the places his fingers had been before dropping off to sleep that night.

Falling.

And maybe I thought about right and wrong, wondered about his age, where he lived, knew somehow that he was lying. Maybe I was just a little bit scared when he took me to Durand Eastman Park and ran his hands up and down my body while I stared into the sun till it burned. Maybe I felt a certain sting when he told me in harsh tones to close my eyes, got angry if I kept them open with his tongue in my mouth.

I knew things.

I had common sense.

I had seen over and over the way men took what they wanted and left women tending the rubble — but none of that mattered, because there I was, after saying no one thousand and forty-nine times; there I was, him on top of me, tongue in my ear, telling me to let go, promising to catch me. He was lying, but I closed my eyes, ate up the coconut of his voice, and fell back onto the motel-room bed.

And that is how I fell.

There.

In that room, moss-green bedspread crumpled at my feet, the air tangy with sweat and mildew, eyes blinded by the white of stiff cotton sheets, stretched under skin the color of raw honey — fingers on my neck, in my pants, wrapped up in my hair.

It was there, eyes closed, hands pushed to the sky, reaching out for something to grab hold of, something that was not there.

109

My mother never made mention of my late arrivals.

She had stopped attending church, and her moods had been more jagged lately—the ups and downs of the past seemed like rolling foothills compared to the cliffs she seemed to scale and fall from daily.

She'd rant about what a pain her children were, how much she wanted us gone. I might come home from school to find all my belongings thrown onto the porch. She'd never say what it was that I'd done, just that she wanted me out.

I stayed out till morning and missed school, but it was never those things that seemed to bother her. Either way, after I'd stayed with Annmarie for a few days, she'd let me back home, the reason for her change of mind as mysterious as the reason for my dismissal.

Most of her free time was spent in bed, wishing everything away. I might come home to a dark house, my younger sisters sitting in front of the downstairs TV or off with friends. Or, more rarely, I might find the house full of light and music, my mother singing while scrubbing vigorously in the kitchen.

This was the case when I arrived after midnight carrying a loaf of French bread, a drunken gift from Ruben. He had insisted on it, pushed his arms round my waist and walked me through the all-night market until I'd chosen just the right thing. I'd pushed away from the beer and cheeses, and headed toward the bakery.

"Ah, aquí está," he said, "here we have it!"

He grabbed a warm loaf of bread and set it in my arms like a baby.

Walking into my mother's kitchen carrying my bread, I saw she was awake, and feared she might ask why I'd been out so late. Instead she only looked at the loaf and asked where it came from. She laughed at my response.

"Ha!" She yelped, and slapped a wet rag to her knee.

She was clearly high and the loaf of bread seemed like comedic genius to her. "That's just the guy we always end up with," she said, "the one who makes a gift of bread."

110

I stood at the living-room window, picking at a thread on a curtain that had begun to unravel, listening to the ups and downs of my mother's voice across the room. She was not high tonight. In fact, she had sounded so low when I'd knocked on her door, I wasn't even sure she'd help.

"Yes," she said into the receiver, and, "I think so."

My gut turned. The pit of my body threatened to twist itself free. I wanted to throw myself onto a bed. But necessity demanded that I stay put, face drawn into the folds of an ugly brown curtain.

My mother had phoned the doctor on call at the Genesee Hospital on my behalf. What started as a normal period had progressed to pain that made me cry out. The tearing in my abdomen was sharp, the lower half of my body throbbed.

She'd been on hold for over five minutes, but finally someone was there, pumping her for information while I picked at the curtain and listened. The sound of her saying my name and date of birth soothed some of the pain I felt, and I had to work to suppress a smile.

My mother's voice was more pointed than usual, more urgent, but the quality of it remained clear, and with her natural cadence, sounded like water running over rocks.

Until the last question.

The energy shifted. She became tentative, her voice lowered as she stretched the cord and ducked into the other room. "Well, I'm not sure," I heard her mutter, and, "I don't think so."

"Hold on," she said, "I'll ask."

I turned to face her, but she didn't meet my eye as she let the words out. "He wants to know if you are sexually active."

Her eyes were on the floor as she spoke, and I turned and continued to pull at the thread.

I'm not sure whether I mumbled or simply nodded, but she stepped into the next room to finish the call, and could not look at me straight for months afterward.

It was the first and last time my mother and I ever discussed my sexual activity. I was seventeen, just finishing my junior year of high school, and doubled over in pain.

111

Seventeen. In that neighborhood, I was practically an old maid. But any victory I'd ever felt for waiting was gone; and all that remained were unanswered questions and my mother's refusal to meet my eye.

They were topics she had not shied away from. Girls we knew — friends of the family and some in the neighborhood — already had babies. She knew I was taking more time getting dressed, spending less time with my friends, and staying out late most nights — so my having sex could hardly have been a surprise. Still, a line had been crossed. There was reality, and there was innuendo. And the saying of it outright took something from us.

Sex. Pregnancy. Men.

What were they to her?

Failure? Freedom? Power?

Paths she followed, but did not prescribe. At least not aloud.

112

I received a call from another doctor a week later, after I'd been treated for what may have been an early miscarriage. After my mother finished that first call, she was silent on the subject and its outcome, and I went to subsequent appointments to the gynecologist on my own.

So when the call came, I answered, and listened as the doctor told me the results of some tests he'd ordered. Endometrium. Progestins. Oligoovulation. The medical terms ran together, but I understood it wasn't good.

I had problems, it seemed, reproductively.

If I ever wanted a child, said the cool voice on the other end of the phone, I might want to get started.

I choked on his words. And a part of me flew away, to the corner of the room, and watched as another girl, a straight-backed stranger, kept her grip on the phone.

"But," I sputtered, "I'm still in high school . . ."

My voice trailed off. Everything slowed.

I couldn't understand why a doctor, of all people, was advising me, a girl from East High School, to have a baby. Was he a purist, simply sharing sound medical advice with a patient, regardless of age and socioeconomic status? Or perhaps he simply did not expect anything else of me.

He ignored my silence and continued to discuss my body as organism — one I had better make use of soon, he said, if I ever intended to.

Since meeting Ruben, I'd been playing with fire, having sex without birth control and going through the monthly drama of praying for my period. But despite my actions, I did not want a child in high school.

I had other plans.

Or did I?

The future could be wonderful, in theory, but the closer it loomed, the murkier it became, the less I knew how to grab hold of it.

113

I didn't know it then, but Chris was every stereotype of gay.

It was the summer between junior and senior year and I was living with Annmarie, who was living with Chris while she waited for her new husband to complete basic training. Chris was a friend from her 7-Eleven job, and his apartment was a place to stay.

At first, I went to the apartment off Monroe Avenue to keep Annmarie company for a few nights. But nights became weeks, then months. Everything was dreary at home, my mother seemed lower than usual, and I couldn't bear another summer of stagnant ghetto heat.

I enjoyed the brightness of Chris's whitewashed walls and Pier One furniture, and couldn't get enough of Chris himself—his tips on the proper application of eyeliner, his stories of love gone south, his stacks of Wham! cassettes.

There were fights. How could there not be? Chris stole my blusher; I broke a champagne glass. Annmarie used up Chris's last squirt of Sun-In; Chris didn't return the twenty dollars he'd borrowed.

But for two whole months, I stayed at Chris's place and pretended I was of the world. We all worked different hours, and many times, I had the apartment to myself, a luxury I'd never known.

I'd sit on the small deck, stretching my legs on the weathered wood beside Chris's collection of potted succulents. I'd read in the company of those desert plants until I got bored. Then I'd slip into black harem pants and walk up and down Monroe Avenue, studying people as they left head shops and used bookstores. The neighborhood was edgy and brooding, a perfect mirror for my own mood.

When Chris was home, we'd slip Madonna into the tape player and spin around the room dancing to "Borderline." We stayed up late talking about men — what made some good, what made some bad — and when I discovered that Ruben had a live-in girlfriend and thought I would split open from the pain of his deceit, Chris held me in his arms and called me *baby doll* while I sobbed under a framed poster of Judy Garland.

114

I cut school and worked more hours, preferring a bigger paycheck to sitting at a desk all day long. I bought new clothes, new shoes, a new winter coat, managed to save enough for spring trips to Florida and California.

Skipping school didn't bother me. Though I'd begged my mother to let me quit Nazareth Academy to attend the public high school in my neighborhood, once there, I found most days at East High uninspiring.

Originally, I'd miss just a day or two to avoid the stifling classrooms and to pad my paycheck. But when I discovered how easy it was and how little it mattered, I began to miss classes more regularly, and by senior year, I was absent most days.

When I wasn't working, I spent my days in bed reading, or riding around glassy-eyed and tired on city busses or strapped into the passenger seat of the banged-up 1968 Volvo that Annmarie had managed to buy.

"Where to today?" I'd ask. And Annmarie would always have a plan. A trip downtown or a drive miles away, depending on our mood and the amount of gas in the tank.

I'd always talked about college and my mother had encouraged me. Clearly, she had not read any parenting magazines or considered the power of self-fulfilling prophecy, because in her mind, the futures of her children were easy enough to figure: Steph was a mechanical genius, and would work on circuitry of some sort; Mal, with her long legs and low grades, might make a good model; Rachel was a reliable helper; and I, with my love of reading and words, would go straight to college after high school. What I'd do in college she couldn't quite say, but that didn't matter so much. It had, for years, simply served as my understood destination.

But as the years of high school passed, and the end came into view, I realized that, for all my mother's talk, no one in my family had ever gone to college. None of us even knew how. As with Janie and the sex-ed filmstrip, the path to college seemed written in a foreign language.

I thought about the future, the blank slate promised to those who made it through high school. My older siblings had gone off to the military, as had others in the neighborhood. And though the military seemed an honest option for kids of limited means, it was not for me. I didn't think I could make it through the physical and emotional rigors of basic training, and had no desire to even try.

I studied people from outside the neighborhood, teachers and people from church, and wondered how they'd managed to go to college. I asked questions, and began to search for anything that might point the way.

The future, which had always gleamed like a treasure I'd been promised, became a heaviness in my pocket. I felt like a five-year-old again with that black snap purse, opening and closing, wondering if I'd ever learn to fill it.

One day while flipping through the pages of a *Mademoiselle*, I came upon an ad for an International School of Fashion Design in Atlanta. The ad featured well-dressed women leaning together over sketches of skirts and dresses, smiling in agreement on the well-cut clothing they would usher into the world. The sun shined in through a tall window. The women glowed. I looked at them for another second, then tore out the attached prepaid postcard.

I'd study fashion, I thought. I liked clothes. But when the call came, my mother took it, and I listened from the living room as she chattered to a woman from the school about her background, her interests, and my bad habits.

"Oh," she said, "I'm from the White Mountains. I'd never be able to live so far south," and, "I'm not sure how she'd do; she's creative, but can be a little touchy."

My mother said the word "touchy" in a loud whisper, then laughed so that by the time the phone was handed my way, I was too ashamed to talk. I mumbled something about calling back, but never did.

Life after high school.

It seemed impossible.

Besides putting outfits together, what else could I do?

I considered nunhood. But while social activism had its appeal, I knew I was not cut out for such selflessness, at least not willingly. And there was the tiny matter of sex.

Languages were another option.

I'd studied Spanish and Italian at school. They were the two classes I'd actually liked, so I sent an application to St. John Fisher, a local Catholic college, and found myself with a plan. For a few weeks anyway. Until the acceptance letter came and with it a request for a deposit.

"Don't look at me," my mother said, as though I'd asked her to walk to the moon and back. And I saw that it was a mystery to her, too. Her intentions were good, but as I looked back over the years and replayed her assurances about college, I realized that it had all been talk.

I began to see just how impossible the whole thing was, and learned to shut down that part of my brain that wanted something different.

115

For the first few months at the Genesee Transportation Council, I colored maps. I felt like an oversized kindergartener as I used thick markers to shade certain areas of Monroe County. Yellow for Parma, red for East Irondequoit, blue for Pittsford.

People would walk by and peek into my workspace, and compliment me on my coloring abilities.

"Nice job there," they'd say, "looks like you really know how to stay within the lines."

They were trying too hard and were corny, but I didn't mind. It was a small office, and the people were friendly. Steph had worked there for a year and recommended me when they needed a part-time clerk.

After the maps were colored, I was handed a counting device, and Steph and I were installed at intersections where we clicked the counter each time a car passed. Then we counted cars in local parking garages.

The projects kept coming.

Over time, Stephanie demonstrated her technical skills and began to work exclusively on computer projects, while I gravitated toward the people end of the transportation business, talking for hours with elderly people on the phone, helping them arrange rides to visit their grandchildren or get to dialysis.

I knew there would be a job for me after high school if I wanted it. Stephanie had moved away from home earlier in the year, but I was able to see her at work, which made my connection to the place even stronger. We'd huddle in the office she had recently scored, swapping stories and laughing.

Karen did the books at GTC. Only a few years younger than my mother, she seemed ages away. Her dark hair was cut into a sleek bob and she spoke openly about her prior marriages, current men, and mixed-up siblings. Karen worked out at the gym during her lunch hour, took vacations to Europe, and wrote stories in her free time.

"I write, too," I told her, and when she offered to read some of the stories of runaway children I'd taken to writing that year, I typed them up and handed them over.

Karen was taking classes at the junior college and encouraged me to consider the same after high school. "I never thought I'd go back to school," she said, "but you owe it to yourself to at least try a class or two."

No matter how rocky things were at home or school, I always showed up at work. Even if I never figured out the future, I knew I'd always have work. Work did not frighten me. Work, I knew.

116

Even on the days I showed up at school, the walls no longer felt real to me. I began to miss more school, weeks at a time.

I took to leaving after my first few classes, or at least by lunch. I'd shove my books into a locker and walk out of the building, counting on the fact that I looked like someone who was doing what she was supposed to be doing. At the large urban school, I was better than invisible; I was a white girl who'd never caused a scene. I'd just breeze out the door, and no one ever seemed to mind. Until a drizzly day in March when a sentry noticed and asked me to stop.

"Where you going?" he asked, fingers strumming the radio strapped to his belt.

I didn't answer. I just kept walking toward the door. I heard him following, could feel him on my heels.

"Hey, girl," he said, "wait up," and, when I did not stop, "just who the hell do you think you are?"

His voice became louder. He cursed to himself and began talking into the fuzz of the radio.

"I'm gonna need some assistance by the main doors."

I walked faster.

I was no real threat, of course, but he couldn't have someone walking away while he was talking. It was a power thing, and I had no choice but to keep walking.

I pushed through the glass doors and saw Annmarie and her old Volvo waiting for me in the loop.

I ran.

The baby blue of my skirt cupped my behind as I stretched my legs toward my friend, who saw me coming and started the engine.

"Don't stop," I said as I slid into the passenger seat. And though another sentry had come from the other set of doors, and two men slapped their hands onto the glass of her windshield, Annmarie put her foot on the pedal and gunned out of the loop.

"What's going on?" she wanted to know.

"Just go," I answered, trying to keep my voice level.

I didn't know what I was doing, but I couldn't stop.

We drove to the mall, where I filled up on cookies and shoes and tried to forget the scene I'd caused back at school. But once the shopping trip was over and I headed toward my job at the transportation council, I worried about what had happened, and half-expected the police to greet me at my job.

I was so afraid of being caught that I missed school for several weeks. The Girls called. Used to seeing me at least a couple times a week, they were worried. Eventually, my worry about failing overtook my fear of arrest, and I was ready to face school again.

I looked both ways as I stepped through the doors of East High and tried to cloak myself in the crowd of students. The sentry was nowhere in sight.

When I didn't see him in between the first few classes, I breathed a bit easier, but still hunched over and made myself as small as possible while walking in the hallways. Until lunch, when I heard that the sentry had lost his job a week prior for trying to pimp out high-school girls.

My relief was thorough, if fleeting.

The boundaries continued to blur.

The following week, I mouthed off to the film studies teacher and was kicked out of class.

"You needed that credit," said my guidance counselor.

Mrs. Wylie had the look of an aging leprechaun. Orange hair leapt from her head and was set off by smiling green eyes. Despite the urgency in her voice, she did not seem overly troubled by my loss of credit. She smiled as though it were just another day, confident that she'd be sipping a gin and tonic by four fifteen, whether someone in her alphabetically-assigned caseload was missing an English credit or not. Still, she tried.

"If you want to graduate," she continued, "you'll have to take an English class at night school."

She leaned in and said this with a wink.

As though we shared a secret. We were partners, it seemed, Mrs. Wylie and I, and as I completed the papers for night school, she softened some, and touched me on the shoulder.

"It'll be fine," she said, "just show up."

117

I was the only kid at night school.

Adults slid behind desks and worked on properly punctuating sentences. When I was handed a ditto to work on, I looked at the Dick and Jane illustrations and turned around to find someone to laugh with. But every other head was bent into the work. My fellow night school students were a serious lot. They came from Laos and Honduras, and when they were not learning to write sentences in English, they kept their eyes on the teacher, moving their bronze faces like sunflowers following a path of light. They wore their pencils into stubs and spoke of a high school diploma with such reverence, I was shamed into working right along with them.

118

You might think that all that time in night school sitting among people who worked ten hours a day, went home to care for children, yet still found time to study sentence structure every evening would have inspired me.

And it did.

You might also think that inspiration led to salvation, as inspiration so often does.

But that's not exactly the way it happened.

Sitting in that room opened my eyes. I was impressed by the motivation of the students, but their drive also served to highlight my own lack of purpose.

Graduation itself had always been a given.

I was smart, why wouldn't I graduate?

But as the end of high school loomed, I began to look around and notice plenty of smart people who hadn't finished high school.

At work, I put my nose to the grindstone.

At home, I spent as much time as I could outside of my house, or hiding under the covers.

And at school, I continued to straddle the line between caring and not caring.

Toward the end of senior year, I walked off the tennis courts during gym class one day with Bernadette Benetti. The sun was shining and we swayed our hips as we crossed East Main Street, taking no pains to hide our AWOL status. We came back a half-hour later, coffee and Danish in hand.

It was a bright day and we felt grown-up as we sipped on coffee from to-go cups.

The PE teacher, Mrs. Rich, had always been attentive, had

encouraged me to go out for the tennis team, but I refused. She said I was good at basketball, too, which was a lie, but a kind one. She was a good teacher. She set limits, but left room for affection. Except on the day Bernadette and I dropped our tennis rackets in favor of coffee.

Mrs. Rich fumed. She called me into her office, where I sat looking at piles of unwashed gym uniforms. Dingy cotton one-pieces in pale blue and sage slopped over the top of an industrial-sized hamper.

She said she had no choice but to fail me. I'd missed so many days already, and just walking off the courts like that showed I wasn't committed to anything.

"Are you?" she asked.

I looked at the dirty laundry and said nothing.

We both understood that this was it. I wouldn't graduate high school without that PE credit.

Mrs. Rich leaned in.

"Well, say something."

I liked the teacher, feared and respected her, but could find no words. When I failed to speak, she scratched a spot behind her ear and said she had no choice but to send me to the dean for suspension.

When I failed to respond even to that, she asked what I did care about anyway. The question had force to it, but even as it hit me, I could find no answer.

119

I went cold as I considered it.

I'd had close calls before. Failing grades. Night school. Missed exams.

Looking back, I wondered when it was I'd stopped trying.

I thought of the bad teachers I'd had. Mr. Burm, who started each English class with a piece of chalk between his fingers. He'd step to the board, scratch out an assignment, then return to his newspaper while we did what we wanted at our desks. I kept waiting for something to happen, long after other students had realized that his class would be just another study hall. What a letdown after the nuns who'd shown such fire while reading poetry.

But there were good teachers, too.

Mrs. Farnham, my eleventh-grade English teacher, for instance. She had Parkinson's or some other ailment that caused her to shake, wore her hair in a quivering pile on top of her head, and made no mystery of the fact that she had only one breast. She loved the books she assigned, and when I actually attended, I found myself touched by Rosasharon's sharing of her milk, could relate to the seasickness of the Joads' westward migration. And who could not visualize Lady Macbeth with those impossible stains on her hands in Mrs. Farnham's telling? Still, I had a job I preferred to school by then. When I received a report card that showed me failing the class, I went to her in a panic. It was a Friday in June, a few days before the end of the school year, but suddenly, I cared. I wanted to pass.

I found Mrs. Farnham in her room, head shaking behind a pile of typed papers. She looked up briefly, then back to her work.

I walked in and stood before her desk.

"I've read some books on my own this year," I said, my voice wet. She'd liked my writing earlier in the year, and I was hoping to impress her with my literary prowess.

"Like what?" she asked without looking up.

I thought hard. I had been reading lots, but didn't think Harlequin romances would impress her. I wanted to show I'd been serious in my choices. I thought of one an English teacher would like: "Well, *Catcher in the Rye*, for starts."

"Outdated piece of shit," she said.

Surprised by the frankness of her opinion, I was unsure whether to try another title or walk away.

Walk away, I decided.

As I started to leave, Mrs. Farnham finally raised her head and asked if I liked feminist science fiction.

Normally I might have laughed, but I was scared and serious for once, so I said I wasn't sure.

She sent me home with a stack of books, told me to have them read by Monday, at which time she kept me after school and asked me to explain the plot, literary approach, and roles of women in each novel.

She was cautious as I began, but showed some satisfaction as I continued. "The female characters are surprisingly strong," I said, "each takes a risk in the novel, and by the end, only one of them seems to regret it."

"Which? And when?" She asked, and leaned in as I answered.

Still, she did not smile.

"I like you," she finally said, "but make no mistake, I am doing you no favor — I would have failed you if you hadn't read every last one of those books."

I thought of Mrs. Farnham and other close calls as I told my mother it looked like I would not graduate from high school. She was in her room, the door closed. I talked through the door and waited for her response as I told her about failing gym class.

She said nothing.

I kept talking.

I said something might happen to save me, but eventually silence hung on both sides of the closed door, and neither of us really believed.

120

"I don't care what the school says, you don't deserve to graduate."

My mother shouted this through an upstairs bedroom window. I was outside, calling the good news up from the street: I would, in the end, be able to graduate.

I was floating, had just come from the Girls' house, where Maritza had shared our news. She'd passed the math exam that had plagued her for years, and Mrs. Wylie had called me down after testing to say that Mrs. Rich, the PE teacher, had made an exception.

"She's letting you pass," the impish counselor reported, looking relieved to have one less student to sign up for summer school.

"Why?" I asked.

She shrugged, said I must have made a good case for myself, but I knew I hadn't. I had apologized to Mrs. Rich for walking out of gym class and ruining her trust, but I had not asked her to change my grade, had spared us both the indignity of my begging.

But she'd changed the grade anyway, my counselor reported and suddenly everyone was happy, hugging me, saying they knew I could do it.

I stood under my mother's window, waiting for her to say something else. It was hot, the sun beating down on me as I waited on the street.

"How'd you trick them into this?" was all she said, her voice sluggish, but clearly angry and disappointed that the school had been duped by the likes of me.

I just stood there, staring up at the window, unable to see her through the sun's glare. I was amazed, almost flattered, by the power my mother thought I had over the school. It was true that I had messed up most of the year, but I had also worked — had walked to and from each and every night-school class.

But I had given up that year, and perhaps in doing so, I'd encouraged my mother to give up right along with me. Still her silence burned more than the late June sun.

Finally, she spoke again.

"It doesn't matter what they say," she said, "you don't deserve to graduate, and I won't have any part of it."

By then, Stephanie was living a few towns away in a tiny apartment with Jimmy Sulli. The older kids were away, and the two younger girls didn't understand what graduation meant, or how close I'd come to not making it.

There was no one to talk to.

My mother slammed the window, and I went in through the front door and let my boxed cap and gown fall to the floor. No tears came. I just lay in the darkened room and nurtured the part of me that believed my mother was right — that I didn't deserve to graduate.

Except for the sound of children playing on the street, the house was quiet. Their laughter drifted in through open windows. My mother and I were rooms away from each other, doors closed, in separate cells, but somehow I had become a replica of her, lying in bed, flattened by the weight of the world.

121

I got up.

The Girls called, said I had to attend the ceremony I'd earned.

"I don't want to," I said.

"There's no way you're missing graduation, white girl." They prodded, and when I complained I had no one to go with, they said I'd go with them.

I stayed in bed.

The Girls called.

Again and again.

"Come on, blanca," they said, "it will be fun," and "we're stopping to see our mother," then finally, that they'd be leaving in forty-five minutes.

I looked at the cardboard box holding the cap and gown, and felt the full drama of the moment.

And finally, I cried.

Over every pain I'd ever felt. Over the imprecise hovering of the future, the nostalgic thorn of the past. Over my mother, my sisters, the father I never knew. Over the places we'd lived, the things we'd lost, and how wilted everything looked just then. Over Ruben and Danny, the doctor's phone call, and the mistakes I'd made.

I sobbed.

And sobbed.

And when my face was as wet as it could get and I was completely cried out, I thought of my mother, huddled a few walls away, and began to feel anger.

She just doesn't want to get out of bed, I realized.

Not for me, or anyone else. She said she wanted the best for us, and a part of her did, but another part just wanted company. She'd never spent a night alone, I remembered her saying. She'd been surrounded by her family, then her husband, and finally us. My mother had had her own collection of pain, and she didn't want to be left alone with it.

I thought of this, and let my anger push me into action. I threw myself into whatever clothes I could find, grabbed the white satin gown and purple tassel, and headed to the Girls' house, bobby pins pressed between my teeth.

The Girls' mother was also in bed — at Park Ridge Hospital, at the end stages of ovarian cancer — but, as promised, we stopped by her room on the way to the school, and I let her kiss of congratulations settle on my skin.

"Soy tan orgullosa," she said, *I am so proud.*

122

I chattered with Maritza as we made our way into the auditorium at East High School. "How's my hair?" I asked, while she begged me to straighten her cap and we stood in line listening to the rules for crossing the stage.

I stuck my head outside and checked the auditorium for someone from my family.

I knew they wouldn't be there, but still I checked.

No one.

"When your name is called, walk to the center of the stage, wait for your graduation partner, then head to the front."

We were to walk out in pairs. Boy and girl.

As names began to be called, I watched as boys in purple gowns and girls in white met at center stage, faced each other briefly, then turned and walked into the limelight. The audience responded with whoops and hollers, hearty clapping, or a polite dribble of applause.

I watched and waited as names were called, and began to fear that no one would clap for me. My friends were there, I knew, but would they make noise?

I considered slinking away.

"Paula Gerace and Tyrone Germaine."

Boys and girls walked onto the stage in smiling pairs, until finally the principal reached the Ls.

"Nilsa Lista and Olivier Lightfoot."

I peeked out again and saw only strange faces.

I knew my name would be next, and steeled myself for the silence I was certain would follow.

"Sonja Livingston and Jonathan Livon."

I walked onto the stage facing Jonny. He was tall and good-looking, a top-notch scholar and stellar athlete. I remembered him from some of my classes, but he'd never looked so golden before. As I approached center stage, I felt a pang of regret that I had not taken my classes seriously.

I moved in what seemed like slow motion to the center of the stage, where light spilled from the ceiling and Jonny flashed a wide smile as we turned to face the audience.

The crowd erupted in whoops and hollers.

People stood and clapped and cheered.

All that light and noise, it felt as though the earth was breaking open.

It took me a second to realize that the thunder wasn't for me — they were cheering for Jonny: star student, golden boy, multiple scholarship winner. They were shouting for him, but I let their light and cheer carry me to the front of the stage just the same.

The crowd continued to crack itself open with applause as I accepted the diploma that had only recently begun to mean something.

Looking out into the packed auditorium, I saw people standing and stomping and shouting for Jonny, but noticed some clapping for me. The Girls. My teachers. Friends. I blinked back the bright lights and felt warm as I exited the stage. I headed toward the stairs, and for a few seconds, let myself enjoy the splendor of the moment, no matter its source. I smiled as I stepped off the stage and felt some of that light making its way into me, and I believed, just then, that I would somehow find a way.

epilogue

Ask anyone who leaves one world for another and you'll hear about a kind of limbo. Once you pass through certain doors, you can no longer go back — you find that your body has grown in ways you could not have predicted, and no longer fits. Even if you sucked everything in and forced yourself through, the rooms you'd find would feel smaller somehow. Constricted.

And still, the place at which you've arrived isn't quite right either. The rooms are wide and light, but you angle your body by habit; manage somehow to sit down to tea, but always, bits of you stick out in ungainly fashion, and you must work to keep yourself in check.

I am grateful for the life I have built, but as with most people, my journey does not end, and I cannot say that I've arrived simply by reaching a place where I no longer worry about how to pay an electric bill.

I managed to make my way. Across that stage at East High School. Through years of college and graduate school. Into a different life. But remnants of the past remain. Like a ghost, the past is always there, flicking its gauzy fingers my way.

I work as a counselor with children, and when I find myself face to face with a six-year-old without lunch money or a nine-year-old whose parents are never home, I feel it. When a friend tells me about a husband who has left, on the perpetual search for something better, I think of my mother, and can almost hear the flapping of wings. When the phone rings at 2:00 a.m., I go cold; it will be the past calling, I know — a sister or brother in need — and as I reach for the receiver, I'm transported back to that small dead end street; standing in that kitchen, staring at the cracked linoleum floor. As though I never left.

Indeed, despite my personal exit from them, the places I came from are still all too real. Western New York remains a place of rampant poverty.

On the reservation, in the rural towns dotting Ontario's southern shore, in the cities of Buffalo and Rochester, boys and girls — even as you read these words — are stuck and struggling to survive. Their families love them, but love is not enough, and so they scour cupboards and backyards and alleyways looking for something more. Children are told that if they work hard, there's a future in store, brighter and better than anything they see. But when they are ready to begin the journey, they find themselves without a map. Or the map they are shown has no local coordinates, and so, wringing their hands, they are left to wonder over points unknown. They may not have the benefit of a lucky break or twist of fate. And they, like all in need, will grab at the first thing that offers itself.

Girls will lie down with sweet-talkers — not because they are stupid or weak, but because they are human beings with hearts and heads and dreams, and above all, hunger, and sometimes sweet-talking is just the thing. They will have babies, because babies are warm and real and maps they can make sense of.

To choose what one knows is so compelling, after all, that one barely realizes she is choosing.

I might have easily become a mother in high school. I could have taken a different and better-marked path, and certainly, I tried for it with my recklessness. Like other girls (and boys) who looked to the future, I saw only a one-sided bridge. Only chance kept me from becoming a parent. Only circumstance allowed me to walk the stage at East High all those years ago. Circumstance, and perhaps a bit of light carried to me by the goodness of others. And it is some combination of such things that brings me to this page.

"How did you make it through?" people want to know. And I am not being humble or coy when I shake my head and can find no words.

I am not sure.

Was it my mother's appreciation for books, access to open fields as a young child, the people at church, a penchant for test-taking, or simply a faulty reproductive system? And I don't wish to condemn where I came from with a celebratory exploration of where I am, and yet, I celebrate.

I celebrate and cry for those who still live in poverty's clutches: beautiful nieces, good-hearted nephews, hardworking siblings. I see with agonizing clarity from where I stand, and though I'd love to point them in new directions, there is no rope strong enough to pull someone from one life to another. And perhaps it is arrogance to try.

Ideals and opportunities and social theorizing are just fine, but if you must understand only one thing, it is this: a warm hand and words whispered into the ear are what we want. Paths that can be seen and followed and walked upon are what we most need.

Because in the end, the thing that feeds us, no matter how tenuous, is what we will reach for.

CPSIA information can be obtained at www.ICGtesting.com
Printed in the USA
BVOW071201130713

325848BV00001B/43/P